# GAME CHARACTER DEVELOPMENT

Antony Ward

**Course Technology PTR**
*A part of Cengage Learning*

COURSE TECHNOLOGY
CENGAGE Learning™

Australia, Brazil, Japan, Korea, Mexico, Singapore, Spain, United Kingdom, United States

# COURSE TECHNOLOGY
## CENGAGE Learning™

**Game Character Development**
**Antony Ward**

**Publisher and General Manager, Course Technology PTR:** Stacy L. Hiquet

**Associate Director of Marketing:** Sarah Panella

**Manager of Editorial Services:** Heather Talbot

**Marketing Manager:** Jordan Casey

**Acquisitions Editor:** Heather Hurley

**Project Editor:** Dan Foster, Scribe Tribe

**Technical Reviewer:** Dan Whittington

**PTR Editorial Services Coordinator:** Erin Johnson

**Interior Layout Tech:** Bill Hartman

**Cover Designer:** Mike Tanamachi

**Cover Illustrations:** Chuck Wadey

**CD-ROM Producer:** Brandon Penticuff

**Indexer:** Sharon Shock

**Proofreader:** Brad Crawford

For product information and technology assistance, contact us at
**Cengage Learning Customer & Sales Support Center, 1-800-354-9706**

For permission to use material from this text or product, submit all requests online at **cengage.com/permissions**
Further permissions questions can be emailed to
**permissionrequest@cengage.com**

Maya is a registered trademark of Autodesk, Inc.

Silo is a trademark of Nevercenter Ltd. Co.

Adobe Photoshop is a registered trademark of Adobe Systems Incorporated.

Library of Congress Control Number: 2008902378

ISBN-13: 978-1-59683-465-5

ISBN-10: 1-59863-465-8

**Course Technology**
25 Thomson Place
Boston, MA 02210
USA

Cengage Learning is a leading provider of customized learning solutions with office locations around the globe, including Singapore, the United Kingdom, Australia, Mexico, Brazil, and Japan. Locate your local office at:
**international.cengage.com/region**

Cengage Learning products are represented in Canada by Nelson Education, Ltd.

For your lifelong learning solutions, visit
**courseptr.com**

Visit our corporate website at
**cengage.com**

Printed in the United States of America
1 2 3 4 5 6 7 11 10 09 08

*These past few months have been difficult. Not only have I been working long hours to write this book, but I also hit a milestone in my career. After 14 years working in house, I decided to go it alone and go freelance.*

*This decision wasn't easy, and if it weren't for the constant support of my wife, Jade, I am not sure whether I would have made the leap. So this book is dedicated to her, my rock and my best friend. I love you.*

*I can't leave it there, though, without mentioning my two little monsters, Jake and Bella. I love you too.*

## Acknowledgments

I admit that the thought of writing another book, of having no free time for at least six months, wasn't immediately appealing. The past few years I had told myself that I couldn't add to my first technical manual or write a sequel because there wasn't enough information to put into another book. That was until I was introduced to the next generation of game development tools.

After submerging myself in these applications, I realized that I could update my first book and share what I had learned with the young game artists out there. To cut a long story short, I set about compiling a table of contents and sent it off to a few publishers.

Heather Hurley, an acquisitions editor at Course Technology PTR, was quick to reply, and through the weeks that followed we worked together to fine-tune the book's content until it was approved.

I had the book idea in place and a publisher waiting for it to be written, but what I needed next was a subject character, something interesting and different than the normal busty female characters so often seen. So at this point I decided to let the public decide, and Chuck Wadey was crowned winner of the online competition I held, allowing me to use some of his amazing Ogre concept art to work from.

Once I began writing, Heather introduced me to Dan Foster, my editor, who worked through my jumbled text with a fine-tooth comb to make it legible.

I want to say a big thanks to all you guys for your parts in bringing this book to life. I couldn't have done it without you!

## About the Author

Since the days when stipple was king, **Antony Ward** has grown with the game development industry, adapting his skills to match its increasing thirst for polygons. During the past 14 years, Antony has led teams, developed workflows, and trained staff in some of today's leading game development studios, all while sharing new techniques as he did with his first book, *Game Character Development with Maya*.

# Contents

# Chapter 6
# UV Mapping    73

# Chapter 7
# Virtual Sculpting    101

# Chapter 8
# Detail Textures    117

# Introduction

The game development industry is in some ways quite similar to the film industry. We create entertainment for the masses, escapism for people as they are taken into different lives, and amazing worlds of imagination and wonder. The outsider's view of what it must be like to work in these industries is often enjoyed through rose-tinted glasses.

I admit, creating characters and seeing them brought to life is an amazing thing. Given the opportunity to be creative, to be in a position where my hobby is also my work, is like a dream come true. I feel lucky to do what I do. I know a lot of people who don't enjoy their jobs; they dread each day, which must be a sad existence especially since we spend most of our lives working.

Unfortunately, the game development industry is not all sugar-coated rainbows; being a game artist does have its tedious times. For example, when you're faced with months of optimization, reducing someone else's work to speed up the game can leave your creative juices running dry. Then there are the bug fixing stages at the end of a project. Imagine having to drive around a track, or search an expansive game world inch by inch to check for a rock that is sticking into the ground just a little too much. It's at these stages in a project when the shine comes off the job, but there is always the next project.

So what about you? Maybe you're already in the game development industry and have acquired this book to brush up on some techniques. Or perhaps you are trying to get a foot in the door of this industry. Whoever you are, I hope you will learn something from this book, and if it holds your hand as you cross the threshold into your first job, then please let me know; it would be very rewarding to think that this book helped someone achieve their dream.

What advice can I then give to an aspiring game artist? When I used to conduct interviews, I didn't look for qualifications. Yes, having them is impressive, but qualifications don't mean much if you don't have the passion and portfolio to back them up. What it always came down to was experience: what the person knew about creating game models and, of course, how good the models were. You could be someone who didn't go to university, someone who knew they wanted to follow this path and spent your time creating game art in your bedroom. This is how I started out, but these days you have a distinct advantage with the Internet and its countless forums and tutorials.

Whatever your background, I say good luck. With practice and confidence you can go far, so polish those characters, pose them, and send them off for review, because you might get lucky.

# Why I Wrote This Book

It's been four years since the release of my first book (*Game Character Development with Maya*) and, as we all know, technology stands still for no one. Although the techniques in my first book are still current and used by many game artists today, it doesn't explore the new generation of character creation tools in depth. If I recall, normal maps are mentioned as an appendix toward the end of the book but are not demonstrated fully.

So I decided it was time to release an update, not replacing my last book but instead enhancing it, so that with both books, you, the artist, could cover all the character creation bases and bring your skills up to date.

My options were to release an updated version of my first book, following in the steps of another famous real-time character book that simply cashed in by releasing the original book with a few extra chapters added on, or I could create a new book, and in this I could develop a new character and show how game artists are adapting their skills to the new technology. As you can guess, I went for the second option—more work, but ultimately more useful to you.

# Why Not Maya Again?

Readers of my first book will no doubt be wondering why this book isn't also dedicated to Maya. The answer is quite simple: back then you could easily use one 3D application to generate your character. Using just Maya (or 3D Studio Max or Softimage XSI), you could create the main character model, apply the UVs, generate various levels of detail, and then go on to rig and animate it. The only deviation would be during the texturing stage when you would dip into Adobe Photoshop.

These days things are a little more complicated, not only in the process but in the choice of tools. With the arrival of normal maps came the need for higher-detailed models—a level of detail so high that to simply model each wrinkle or crease would add weeks to an artist's schedule. Once this model was created, the artist would also need to extract the detail in the form of a texture, something that can give varying results depending on the software used. Luckily, technology has come to our rescue in the form of virtual sculpting applications. These take a basic model and allow the artist to literally paint the detail onto the mesh, deforming its surface by pushing, pulling, scratching, or smoothing with each brush stroke. Working this way not only helps create superior quality models but does so at a fraction of the time.

As you can see, the steps taken to create a character have grown. Now you need to create a base mesh and take it into a sculpting package to paint in the detail. With both the high- and low-resolution mode, you then need to extract various maps, including a normal map. It's only after all this that you can settle into a single application and work on the actual game model.

At the moment it simply isn't possible to do all these steps in a single piece of software, but maybe with Autodesk's acquisition of Skymatter (the creators of Mudbox) that will change. Some applications do have the ability to sculpt, but these features often feel bolted on as an afterthought and as a result aren't as easy to use as the stand-alone packages. Nor do they have the same amazing tools. For now, we are left using at least one 3D application, one sculpting application, and, of course, a 2D application for texture work.

Throughout this book you will see how using separate tools can actually be beneficial. New smaller applications are coming into the mainstream that offer faster, more intuitive ways to model and texture, so it's not always a good idea to be loyal to a single application. Of course, cost does factor into things, but with Silo costing a mere $150, it's worth it to make your life easier.

# What This Book Covers

What will you find in this book and how does it differ from my first book? Well, most of *Game Character Development with Maya* is still relevant, especially the areas that cover the later stages of character creation. What this book aims to do is expand upon the first, taking everything you learned in that and pushing it to the next level—or next generation.

Throughout this book you will see how to create a high-detail character. We will begin by looking at new modeling techniques before creating our base mesh. With a base mesh complete, we will then apply UV data before I introduce virtual sculpting. Once we have the detail model created, we will then explore advanced texturing techniques before finishing by optimizing the main mesh.

Once the character is complete, you can then refer back to my first book to see how to tackle level of detail models, character rigging, and even animation.

# Applications and Companion CD

As you have probably worked out by now, this book has been written such that it's not specific to any application. Where possible, I have kept the instructions generic so they can be applied to any 3D program, but where relevant I have given a brief introduction to the tools I chose to use, and why I use them.

Also to help you as you progress, you will find various files on the companion CD, all of which were exported in the Wavefront OBJ file format, which is a universal file format that can be imported into many, if not all, major 3D applications.

# 1

# Subdivision Surfaces

Before we rush in and begin creating our character, it's probably a good idea to start by looking at what we're working with. Rather than focus on the more fundamental areas of 3D, like polygons and vertices, we will jump ahead and examine subdivision surfaces.

Also known as limit surfaces or Sub D's, subdivision surfaces have been around for a while now and are widely used for creating high-end 3D models, but understanding them, and their construction, can prove useful to current-generation game development.

Don't worry; this chapter won't be an in-depth look at algorithms and theories but more a general look at this approach to modeling.

## What Are Subdivision Surfaces?

Hardware is ever changing. Processors increase in speed, and with each generation graphics cards are able to throw around more polygons, but as their power grows, the restrictions forced onto game artists relax, allowing them the freedom to be more ambitious.

As it stands, working on a highly detailed model comprised of many millions of polygons is a nightmare, not only for the hardware but also for general manipulation. Subdivision surfaces give the artist the freedom to focus on a low-resolution model, known as a cage, base, or control mesh, safe in the knowledge that a simple button or key press will convert it into a smoother, higher-resolution model that in turn can be worked further by manipulating the control mesh.

Figure 1.1a shows an example of a control mesh. This is the rougher, more angular model that is built initially.

Figure 1.1b then shows the model converted to a subdivision surface. Notice how nice and smooth it is, but what you will also see is the wireframe from the base mesh traced across its surface showing its origins.

Finally, in Figure 1.1c, the subdivision surface model has been baked back into polygons. When comparing this to the previous model, you can see how much denser the mesh is, meaning it would be more difficult to edit or manipulate.

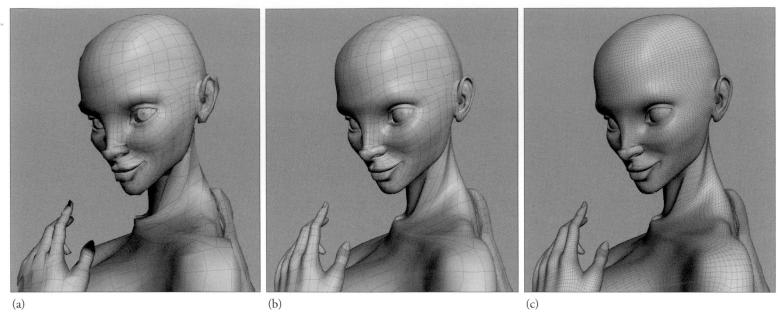

(a)                                        (b)                                        (c)

**Figure 1.1**  The control mesh (a), the subdivision model (b), and the baked polygon model (c).

# How Do Subdivision Surfaces Work?

Well, in layman's terms, all that happens is that the surface of the control mesh is subdivided—hence the name. New vertices and faces are added with their position calculated using the original vertex positions and one of two refinement schemes. Figure 1.2 shows a simple cube with two subdivision passes applied. One pass will convert a quad into four, a second will convert each of the new four into a further four, and so on.

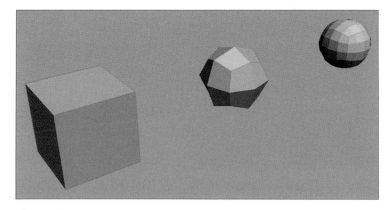

**Figure 1.2**  A simple cube with two refinements applied.

There are two subdivision schemes: Approximation and Interpolation (Figure 1.3). Popular applications like Maya, 3D Studio Max, Silo, and Softimage XSI rely on an approximation algorithm called Catmull–Clark. This algorithm was created by Edwin Catmull and Jim Clark in 1978—a creation that landed Edwin, the current president of Walt Disney Animation Studios and Pixar Animation Studios, an Academy Award in 2006 for Technical Achievement.

The two schemes differ in that Interpolation will try to retain the original shape of the mesh. With each division, the vertices will stick closely to the their parents, which gives a more predictable result but can come at the cost of the overall appearance because bulges can occur if the base mesh is complicated. Approximation, on the other hand, will give a smoother surface with the only cost being its resemblance to the original shape.

See, that wasn't full of technobabble, was it?

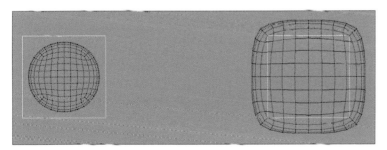

**Figure 1.3** A cube with Approximation (left) and with Interpolation (right) refinement applied.

# Hard Surfaces

You can see how this method of modeling can be great for organic models such as characters or creatures, but what about harder surfaces or man-made objects?

Let's look at a basic cube (Figure 1.4a). If we subdivided this cube, it would turn into a sphere, right? You can see this in Figure 1.4b.

What we can do is "crease the edges"; this will tell the 3D package that the edges need to remain unsmoothed. Creasing just the top edges of the cube gives us the result in Figure 1.4c, whereas creasing all the edges will cause the object to try and retain its original shape (Figure 1.4d).

Figure 1.4e shows our subdivided cube converted back into polygons, so you can see where new edges and vertices were added.

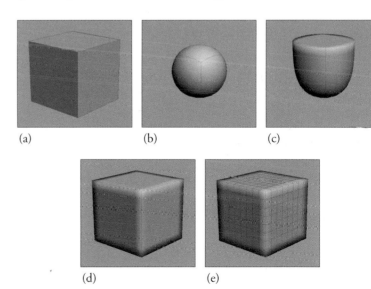

(a)          (b)          (c)

(d)          (e)

**Figure 1.4** An example of using creases to retain hard edges in a subdivision surface model.

## Surfaces Memory

Working with subdivision surfaces gets better. Even when we've converted the model into a subdivision surface, we can still work on the control mesh, viewing any modifications we make in real time as they move up the chain and affect the smoother model (see Figure 1.5).

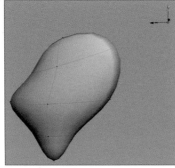

**Figure 1.5** Moving a vertex on the control mesh will instantly update the smoother, higher-detail version.

This can result in a fast and intuitive way of working on what is a low-resolution mesh in a high-detail model's clothing.

## Why Is Subdivision Surface Modeling Useful for Real-Time Models?

Modeling this way can help the artist to generate multiple levels of the same model, often called *levels of detail* (LOD). The LOD are switched in the game engine so that as a character moves away from the camera and becomes smaller on screen, a model with less detail is used, saving precious processing power.

To the artist, creating these variations could mean simply using different subdivision steps, with a minor amount of optimization.

Another use is the ability to create a high-detail model quickly and easily that can then be used for normal map generation. Using subdivision surfaces will give you two models for the price of one; you end up with a low-resolution target model and a higher-detail source model, which could also be sculpted upon for finer details.

This brings us nicely to another plus point, centered around virtual sculpting. We will go into this as well as normal map generation later in the book, but to successfully sculpt a model, you first need to subdivide it correctly. Knowing how to construct your model is important; if the topology is wrong, you could end up with unwanted pinches and creases in your subdivided mesh that would be near impossible to remove.

Now you should have an understanding of subdivision surfaces and their possible uses. In the next chapter we will look into model topology and explore edge loops, poles, and the various approaches to building your character.

# 2

# Model Construction

When creating a model with the intention of taking it into a sculpting package, as we will do with this book, you have to take a different approach.

In this chapter we will look at the various elements used in mesh construction before moving on to the variety of methods artists use to create their models.

## Mesh Topology

There is a strict set of rules that needs to be followed when creating any real-time model. The topology has to be clean, it must be well optimized, it should deform convincingly, and, if possible, the silhouette must not show any angular edges.

A game model—whether constructed from quads, triangles, or a mixture of both—is converted to triangles upon export, or at render time, meaning artists are free to build as they please. But a model destined for subdivision must be approached differently. In most cases, such a model must be quad-based to maintain a predictable refinement and to avoid unwanted surface artifacts.

In this section we will take a close look at the key elements of a model, expanding on the fundamental polygons, triangles, and vertices with which you are more than familiar.

## Edge Loops

There is a lot of discussion on the Internet about edge loops and how best to explain them to a novice modeler. I have read many articles and have worked extensively with edge loops myself, so here is my brief take on them.

Edge loops are quite simply the flow of edges on an object's surface. The placement of these edges dictates how the object will subdivide and how it will deform when animated. If edges are cleverly placed, the result will be a highly efficient model.

Imagine taking a pen and drawing a grid over your body, but with this grid you follow the natural contours and muscles of the figure. Each of these lines is essentially an edge loop, with each square on the grid being a quad.

Translate this into 3D, and you will have your perfectly "quaded" model.

## Muscle Lines

I touched upon muscle lines in my first book—how placing your edges to follow the lines of the muscles will allow your model to deform convincingly. The same applies here, and is even more important.

Tracing the muscles of the body with edge loops is a key part of model construction. Once it is subdivided, the edge loops will help add subtle details to the surface and, when animated, the model will bend, stretch, and crease in a more realistic way.

The head in Figure 2.1 demonstrates how having the edge loops constructed along muscle lines makes it easier to pose, gives a more natural look when animated, and ultimately gives better results.

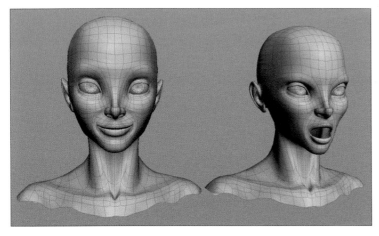

**Figure 2.1** Well-placed edge loops allow for easy manipulation in models intended for animation.

## *n*-Gons and Poles

3D models are made up of edges, vertices (or points), and faces (polygons). Traditionally a polygon was a four-sided face, but these days most applications and game engines support the use of polygons with more than four sides. These are commonly known as *n*-gons (Figure 2.2).

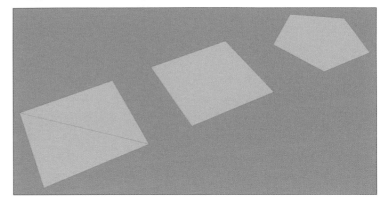

**Figure 2.2** A triangle, quad, and five-sided face (*n*-gon).

Another element to consider is a "pole." As illustrated in Figure 2.3, a pole is a vertex with more than four edges coming into it. These are usually not good to use, since subdividing will create a dense collection of polygons around the pole, causing the surface to pinch. They are also frowned upon in game engines because they can increase render time, making your model inefficient.

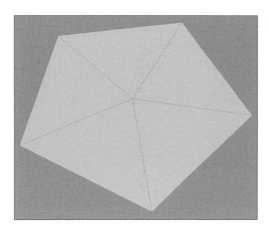

**Figure 2.3**

An example of a pole.

It's difficult to create a game model based purely on quads, so *n*-gons and poles are unavoidable, but keeping them to a minimum or tucking them away is a good idea if you cannot remove them completely.

Figure 2.4a illustrates how a quaded mesh will subdivide in a predictable and acceptable way so the surface remains smooth.

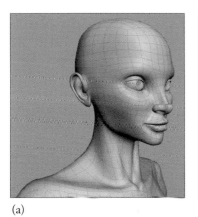
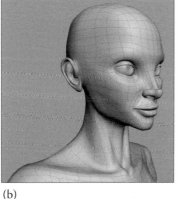

(a)                              (b)

**Figure 2.4** A quad-based mesh versus a mesh housing *n*-gons and poles.

The model in Figure 2.4b holds obvious poles and *n*-gons in her cheek, each interrupting the contours of the surface and resulting in unwanted creases and pinches.

In short, keeping your model clean and tidy is always a good thing.

## Modeling Methods

Many methods exist for creating characters, and as time passes artists find innovative and faster ways to construct their models. Following are some of the more common approaches.

### Point by Point

This approach to modeling involves duplicating existing vertices, or points (Figure 2.5b), before building polygons between them (Figure 2.5d). The mesh is then built up gradually, meaning this method is more time consuming yet more precise if you are working from an image plane or reference image.

### Extruding

A step up from point by point, extruding concentrates on edge manipulation. As you can see in Figure 2.6, the edges are extruded to create the desired shape; the vertices are then tweaked to refine the surface.

### Box Modeling

One of the more popular modeling approaches is box modeling. The artist usually begins with a standard primitive such as a cube and extrudes the faces to build up the basic shape (Figure 2.7). This is then worked further by splitting edges and adding edge loops to achieve the desired shape.

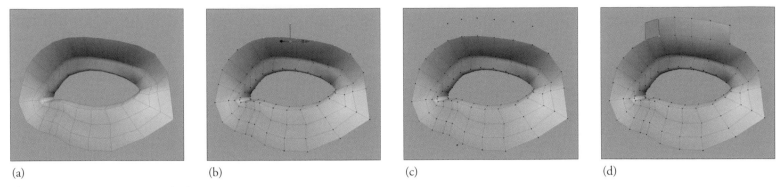

(a)        (b)        (c)        (d)

**Figure 2.5** The eye is built by duplicating points.

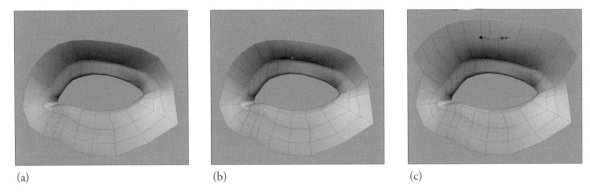

(a)        (b)        (c)

**Figure 2.6** Edge extruding to create the model.

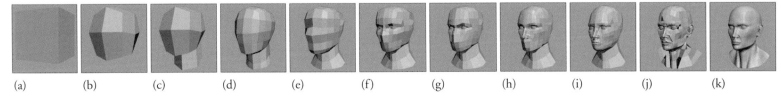

(a)   (b)   (c)   (d)   (e)   (f)   (g)   (h)   (i)   (j)   (k)

**Figure 2.7** A box-modeled head. The final image shows the mesh smoothed.

# Sculpting

Unlike the previous methods, sculpting doesn't involve direct mesh manipulation. The artist begins with a base mesh, quad based and generated to be subdivided. This is then taken into a sculpting package like Mudbox or ZBrush, and the surface is pulled, pushed, and pinched to achieve the detail needed (Figure 2.8). This is fast becoming the primary method for generating highly detailed models because it is quick and simple.

**Note**

If your budget is tight, don't worry; both Maya and 3D Studio Max have their own built-in sculpting tools, although they are not as nice to use. Even better, Silo allows users to sculpt their models at a very reasonable price of around $150.

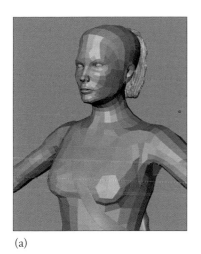
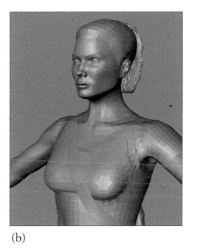
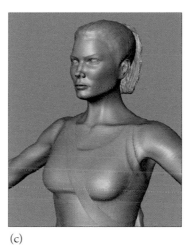

(a)     (b)     (c)     (d)

**Figure 2.8** A sculpted figure. With each refinement more detail is added.

# Resurfacing

Sometimes you need to move backwards. If you have a dense model holding millions of polygons or your current game model has bad topology, what do you do? Many moons ago a small package called Silo introduced the modeling world to the Topology Brush (Figure 2.9). With this tool, you could take your model and literally paint onto its surface, marking out how you would like the topology to be on a low-resolution base mesh. Once finished, these lines would be turned into polygons like magic for you to take aside and use as a start for a new game model.

The Topology Brush has since been expanded upon, and now most modeling packages have similar tools. Their approaches vary, but each achieves a highly organized model.

The "theory chapters" are now over; hopefully you now have a basic knowledge of modeling methods and a preview into some of the techniques we will look at in this book.

Let's move forward now and look at the character we will create in this book, and his origins.

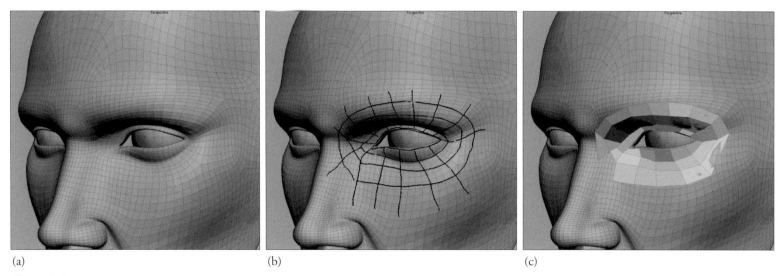

(a)                                    (b)                                    (c)

**Figure 2.9** Silo's Topology Brush

# 3

# The Character You'll Create: The Ogre

I decided to take a different approach with this, my second book. I could have rehashed the character Kila from my first book, slapping on a normal map and adding a few polygons—minimum work that would have resulted in a new book. I didn't want to do this. A new approach needed a new book, plus I wanted the character I created to be one that people wanted to see, rather than going with the typical femme fatale or mech-soldier.

So now I will introduce you to the creature you are about to make, and explain its origins.

## About the Ogre

To model a creature that the public wanted to see, I decided to turn to the online computer graphics community and hold a competition. I asked willing concept artists to submit their ideas, which I then collated and narrowed down to a final four.

These finalists were then uploaded to the Internet for the public to vote on. Figure 3.1 shows the winning entry, with 48.57% of the votes.

## About the Artist

Chuck Wadey is a professional freelance illustrator currently working from his home studio in Austin, Texas. He graduated from the Art Center College of Design in 2001 with a degree in Illustration and has since been working as a concept artist for the video game and entertainment industry.

Chuck worked on the Spider-Man franchise games for Activision, and his artwork has been published in two Brady Games Spider-Man strategy guides, the journal *Nature*, and *ImagineFX* magazine. Chuck works primarily in digital media and specializes in traditional and digital drawing and painting, character design, prop and vehicle design, environmental design, background painting, storyboarding, modeling turnarounds, and level layout.

To find out more or to contact Chuck Wadey, go to www.chuckwadey.com or www.myspace.com/chuckwadey.

# Why I Chose the Ogre

I personally like this model because it will help me cover most areas of character creation. The Ogre has good muscle tone, clothing, fur, hair, and interesting features. I like the fact that he isn't human, as it will give us the opportunity to experiment with wrinkles and skin effects as we sculpt his leathery, aged skin.

I am sure an attractive female would have helped sell the book, but she wouldn't have offered us this variety in surface detail and elements.

**Figure 3.1**

The Ogre by Chuck Wadey

# 4

# Model Preparation and Recycling

With subdivision surfaces and modeling techniques behind you, and with a clear view of the character you are about to make, we can now start to focus on the project at hand.

But before you begin to create this beast, it's important to take a breath and plan your approach.

## Model Preparation

We have our concept, but this doesn't mean we are ready to begin modeling. To start off on the right foot, we also require a model sheet (Figure 4.1).

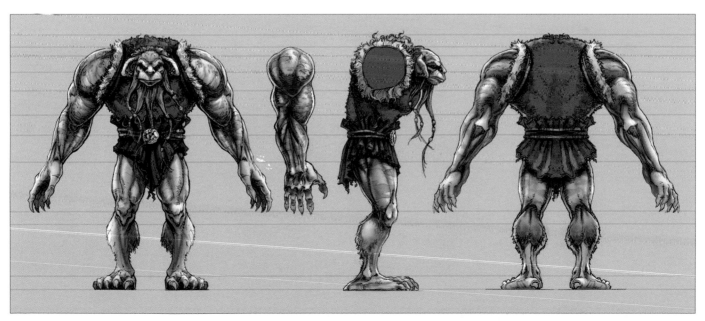

**Figure 4.1**
The Ogre model sheet.

The model sheet is an essential piece of artwork that will guide us as we build the foundations of the character, helping us maintain its proportions and form. This blueprint shows us the Ogre from three main angles—front, back, and side—which means creating him will take little guesswork on our part.

What it also allows us to do is to break down the character into manageable chunks, making the task of modeling him less daunting. As you can see in Figure 4.2, this particular character

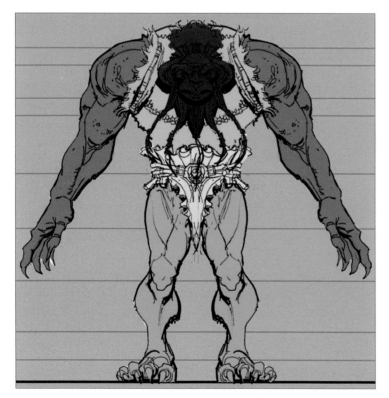

**Figure 4.2** The Ogre divided into manageable elements.

can be divided into his head, arms, legs, and clothing. If we wanted, we could separate the character further, highlighting his belt, beads, and hair, but at this early stage this should suffice.

It is also good to have detail shots of the character. These are close-up sketches showing details in key areas, giving the artist even more to work with, and resulting in a finished character that is exactly as the concept artist intended. Luckily, our model sheet holds all the detail we will need.

# Researching Your Character

Working straight from the concept and detail shots is a good starting point, but it's never enough. It would be a good idea to spend some time initially researching the different elements of your character.

So, your first task in this book is to open up your Web browser and start searching for reference material on items like the following.

## Muscles

Start with the basics; stripping the Ogre bare would reveal his toned physique, so begin by hunting for good muscle photos to work from. www.3d.sk is a good site to try; it has some fantastic photos and is an essential stop for reference.

Also try looking on CG forums such as www.cgtalk.com, www.tweakcg.com, or the ZBrush or Mudbox forums. Lots of people post their work and the majority will be of highly toned men or creatures. These are great reference sites because people often post images with various angles, and it's always handy to see a figure from all sides. Just make sure the images you use are accurate, as some people may get the muscles slightly wrong or even exaggerate them.

At the end of the day, nothing beats a good photo reference. You can find plenty on the web, or, if you have some spare cash, you could get a good anatomy book.

For a list of good web sites and books, please see the Reference appendix at the end of this book.

## Clothing

Next we have his clothing. His top appears to be made from fur, so hunt out some primitive-aged clothing. You might search for Neanderthal clothing before looking for images of fur coats.

His loin cloth is more than likely fashioned from leather, so you need leather references as well as loin cloth images to work from. The folds are a different story; trying to create these from your imagination will be tough, so it would be a good idea to refer to photos or traditional sculptures and examine how they depict cloth.

## Face

This character has a very interesting face. He has slightly human features combined with what appear to be features of a gorilla or an ape. To create a believable face, we need to hunt out references that will help us sculpt the deep wrinkles and creases that would have formed throughout his life.

Again, creating these from memory may not be the best approach, so find plenty of reference material to work from.

## Other Character Features

What else could you look for? Well, you could search for hair, or more examples of skin to refer to when you work on his arms and legs. You might go further and gather some images of finger and toe nails, handmade jewelry, and even teeth.

At this early stage, more reference material is better than none; without images to refer to, you may find yourself stumbling ahead blindly. This will only result in your having to revisit the model at a later date and redo areas before he is finished.

# Real-Time Game Model Restrictions

Unlike traditional 3D artwork, models created for use in games need to adhere to a strict set of rules. If you imagine your console is an empty box, there is only so much you can fit into it before the sides burst. With games, the box is restricted by its hard drives, processors, and memory. They can only display a certain amount of polygons and textures at a time and if you add to those essential effects like reflections, water, and atmospheric effects, the space is soon filled.

Your polygon and texture budget must be divided among the environment, characters, props, and effects, so the amount allowed for our character depends greatly on the game and the target platform. If this were a fighting game in which the focus was on the characters, we could possibly go wild and have 30,000 to 40,000 polygons (if developing for the Xbox 360, Playstation 3, or PC). For this book, however, we will stick to a traditional third-person action game, similar to *Gears of War, Mass Effect*, or *Resident Evil 5*, where you see the game from behind the character. This being the case, we will restrict ourselves to 15,000 triangles—maybe 20,000 if we need them for extra detail.

As for texture pages, its generally better to work larger from the outset as it's much easier to reduce a page than to try to enlarge it later. We will work to two 2K color maps (that's two pages that are 2048 x 2048). This may not seem like much, but you have to remember that each page will ultimately be accompanied by a normal map, a specular map, and, depending on the game engine, this could also include an ambient occlusion map and maybe even a few others (which are covered in Chapter 9, "Texture Building").

# Recycling Previously Created Models

Any good digital artist will have a stock of models stored away to call upon when he needs them. These could be body parts like hands or ears, which when modeled once can be applied to any character, saving precious time.

Another asset to keep hold of is a well-built base model. This is a basic, fully quaded mesh that can be taken into a sculpting application and molded into any character. Figures 4.3, 4.4, and 4.5 show three example models.

The first (Figure 4.3) is one I was given by a friend I used to work with. It gives a great starting point for generating a male character in Mudbox or Zbrush. From here it's simply load and sculpt.

Next (Figure 4.4) is one I created from Zack Petroc's DVD titled *Digital Sculpting: Human Anatomy*. Although this is basic compared to the previous model, it has excellent topology for subdividing and sculpting, as Zack expertly shows in his tutorial.

Finally (Figure 4.5) is another I created for a personal project.

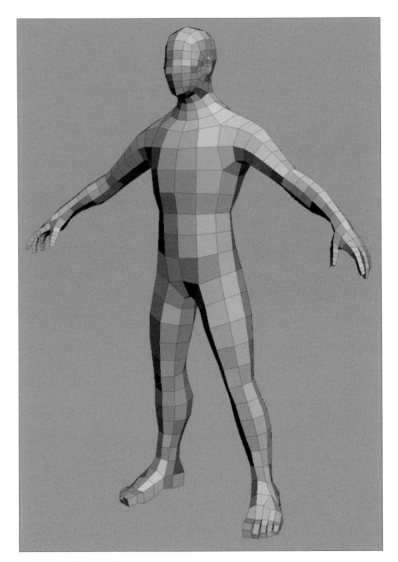

**Figure 4.3** A quaded base model

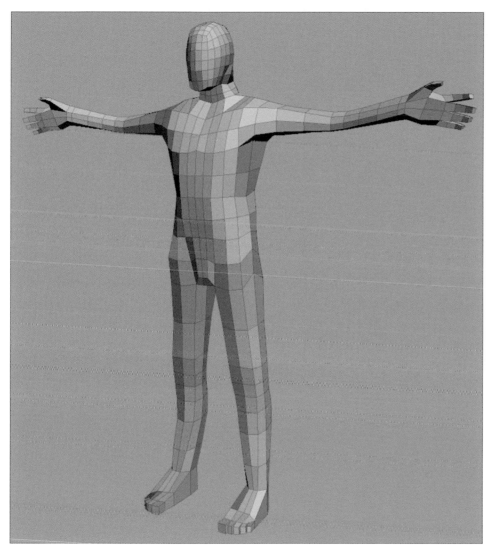

**Figure 4.4** The Zack Petroc base mesh from *Digital Sculpting: Human Anatomy*

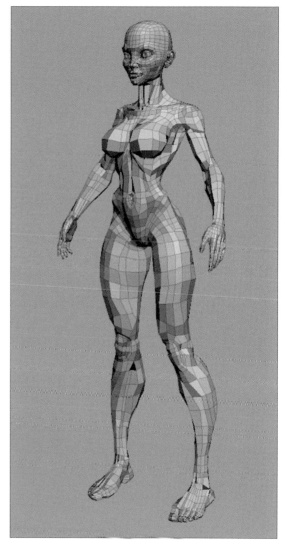

**Figure 4.5** A stylized female base model

This character has much more detail than the previous two but is a great starting point for a real-time model. The addition of facial features and basic muscle tone could remove the need to resurface or rebuild the base mesh after the detail pass is added. With the other models, rebuilding the base mesh would be inevitable as it would eventually need these details included.

Neither approach is right or wrong; which is used comes down to how the artist is comfortable working, although many artists use the very basic base meshes when generating characters for rendering, where they will be posed and used for a still image.

My advice would be to keep models as you create them; you never know when you may need them again. There is no point in reinventing the wheel, so if you have a good model, reuse it.

# Getting Feedback

It's essential to get feedback on your work. After spending a week sculpting tiny details into a mesh, you become blind to the bigger picture. A fresh pair of eyes makes a hell of a difference, especially if they are experienced.

This is especially encouraged when you are working as part of a team, since good constructive criticism can not only help you with problem areas, but can also reignite your interest in the project.

What if you work from home or you don't have access to experienced people? The online computer graphics community is expanding every day. Many forums spring up that are soon flooded with people sharing their work and seeking advice. Here are a few I frequent.

www.cgtalk.com

www.gameartisans.org

www.subdivisionmodeling.com

www.tweakcg.com

Don't be shy; post a few screen grabs and let the community help you.

# Approach

With all this considered, let's now think about how we should approach creating this character model. The traditional approach for previous consoles like the Xbox or Playstation 2 is straightforward and would be as follows.

1. Build the main mesh, adding all the detail into it including facial features, clothing, and so on.
2. Optimize the model, removing unused and unseen polygons.
3. Apply UV data to the character so we can add a texture.
4. Paint the color, specular, and bump maps in an art package.
5. With the model in the game engine, tweak the textures until you are happy.

There is nothing wrong with this approach and it has provided some amazing characters, but for a true "next-gen" creature, you will need to take this process further.

1. Create a basic quad-based mesh. No detail needs to be added at this stage; it just needs to fit the general form of the character.

2. Take this base mesh into a sculpting package and work in the detail pass. This could even see you adding minute details like pores in the skin.

3. Extract the base mesh and rework it, or use the higher detail model as a reference as you create a new base model. This will be done using the topology brush or similar resurfacing tools.

4. Apply UV data to the new base mesh.

5. Extract a normal map using the new base mesh and the sculpted, detail model.

6. Now it's time to paint those textures.

7. With textures done, take the character into the game engine and play around with the textures and in-game shaders until you are happy.

This is the process we are going to follow in this book, so each step will be discussed in more detail as we proceed.

Now it's about time we stopped talking and started doing—with the turn of a page we will pass from theory into practice and begin building our base mesh.

# 5

# Building Foundations

With the theory over, it's time to get your hands dirty and start modeling. In this chapter we concentrate on the base mesh and fleshing out the basic proportions and shape before moving on and adding UV data in the next chapter.

## Silo

As mentioned in the introduction, this book is written in such a way that it doesn't focus on any particular modeling application, making it easier for anyone to pick up and follow regardless of preferences. I will, however, share with you the tools that I will be using, and explain why I use them.

To begin, I am going to use Silo. Here is the description from their website, www.nevercenter.com:

> *Silo 2 is a focused 3D modeling application with the ability to effortlessly switch between organically sculpting high-polygon models and precisely controlling hard-edged surfaces. It can be used for anything from creating 3D characters for video games and movies to quickly exploring 3D architectural ideas.*

*Silo is currently being used at top studios worldwide as both a stand-alone design tool and as a versatile element of a multi-software 3D graphics workflow. It is available for both Windows and Mac OS.*

I have been using Silo for over a year now. It's a fantastic modeling package that hasn't got all the bells and whistles larger applications have, meaning you don't need to jump through hoops to select an edge. Its streamlined interface and hotkeys are completely customizable, and the speed with which I can work in it means I can create a model in half the time it would take me using Maya.

You will find a trial version of Silo on the accompanying CD.

Now you know that I'll be using Silo, let's begin modeling. But remember, you can use any modeling application as you work through this chapter.

# Creating the Basic Shape

The way I like to approach a model isn't like any mentioned in Chapter 2. As you will see, I prefer to begin with cylinders as I block out the basic shape. I do this because our arms and legs are basically cylinders, so using cylinders is like giving yourself a head start. In this section we will block out the limbs and torso, stitching them together before we move on to create his extremities.

## Preparing Your Scene

Before you do anything, it's important to verify that you are working in the correct units of measurement. These dictate the scale you will be working to—usually centimeters or meters. Check with your project lead and adjust your scene accordingly. At this early stage this isn't a major concern, but it's better to start the project in the same way as you mean to follow through with it.

Many people like to throw themselves into the 3D world, using their imagination and visual judgment to help them build their characters. For some people this works well, but these people tend to be extremely experienced in all matters of anatomy such that judging proportions and surface tone comes naturally.

For us, and many other artists, we need some solid reference to work on top of. For this we can use the model sheet, bringing it into our application so it can guide us.

1. First take the image file OgreModelsheet.jpg and divide it up so you have three main files for front, back, and side. (You will find these already divided on the companion CD.)

   Most images can be too bright, meaning that when you bring them into your 3D application you lose your wireframe. To help see your mesh as you model, it might be worth dimming the images first in your preferred 2D package.

2. Next bring these files into your application, assigning them to the appropriate views (see Figure 5.1). I prefer to use image planes, but feel free to use whichever method you are more comfortable with.

> **Note**
>
> It's important to make sure the images are all the same size so you're not chasing your tail as you switch between the different views.

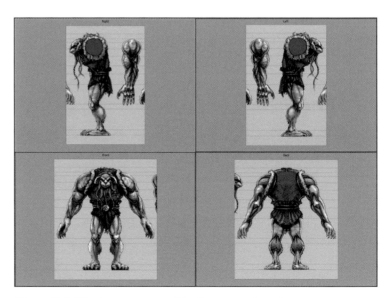

**Figure 5.1**  The images arranged in the appropriate views.

That's our scene pretty much ready; there wasn't much to do but it's good to make the proper preparations. Now let's begin modeling.

## Arms

When creating a new character I always begin with the arms. I'm not sure why—perhaps it helps to give a sense of proportion, or maybe it's because the arms are a main part of any character. Either way it's as good a place as any, so let's jump in.

**Note**

At this stage we can rely on creating one side of our character, since he is more or less symmetrical. This will save us doing twice the work because we can just duplicate and mirror one side later.

1. Switch to the front view and create a cylinder. As in Figure 5.2, create the cylinder with 10 subdivisions around its axis and 10 along its surface.

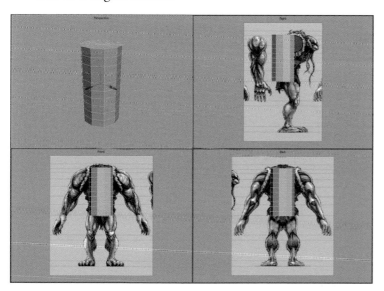

**Figure 5.2** Create a basic cylinder.

2. As demonstrated in Figure 5.3, first position the cylinder so it lies over the arm on the model sheet, making sure you also match its orientation.

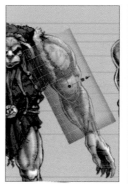

**Figure 5.3** Scale the cylinder in the front view to match the arm in the image.

3. Next, using a global scale, select each horizontal edge loop (the loops of edges going around the arm) and scale them to match the arm.

4. Finally, adjust the edge loops at the top of the arm so it bends toward the torso.

5. Switch to the side view now, and this time scale only horizontally (front to back). We do this so we won't affect how the arm looks from the front (see Figure 5.4).

That's the basic arm blocked out, which is really all we need at this stage, so let's move on and give him a leg.

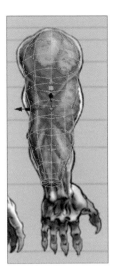

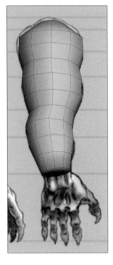

**Figure 5.4**

Scale the cylinder in the side view to match the arm in the image.

**Figure 5.5**

Scale the horizontal edges of the cylinder to match the leg in the image.

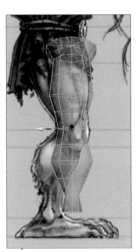

**Figure 5.6**

Adjust the cylinder from the side to match the image.

# Legs

To create the legs we will use exactly the same procedure as with the arms.

1. Switch back to the front view now and create another cylinder, positioning it over the Ogre's leg as shown in Figure 5.5. Make sure this has the same configuration as the arm cylinder.

2. As with the arm, globally scale each edge loop to match the shape of the leg in the image. Make sure to rotate the upper loops so they tilt toward the pelvis.

3. Working from the side now, scale the edge loops again to match the leg remembering to scale only along the horizontal axis. In this instance though, you may want to rotate each loop so it follows the contours of the leg, as in Figure 5.6.

The limbs are complete; now let's work on his upper body.

# Torso

We will now move on to the main trunk of the Ogre, but this time we will use a higher-resolution cylinder as our starting shape.

1. Create a third cylinder, but, as shown in Figure 5.7, this time it needs to have 20 divisions around its circumference. This is because we will eventually halve it, leaving it with the same number of divisions as the arm and leg, making it easier to stitch the elements together.

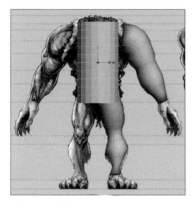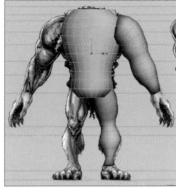

**Figure 5.7** Create a higher-resolution cylinder as the base for the torso and globally scale each horizontal edge loop.

2. Scale each horizontal edge loop so the shape roughly matches that in the image.

3. For the last time, switch to the side view and scale, and then rotate each edge loop to match the curvature of the Ogre's spine (see Figure 5.8).

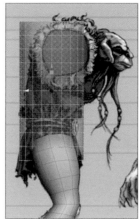

**Figure 5.8**

Finally, scale the torso to match the Ogre's torso, matching the curvature of his spine.

You should now have a very basic torso, leg, and arm like those in Figure 5.9. We can't leave these elements separate, however, so next we will look at combining and merging them together to create a single, seamless mesh.

> Now is a good time to save. For reference you can find the file Ogre_01.obj on the companion CD.

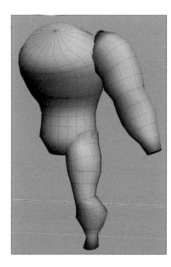

**Figure 5.9**

The basic torso, leg, and arm of our Ogre.

# Combining Elements

Before we begin to seamlessly attach these elements we need to remove some geometry. We do this both to make way for the connections and to remove any redundant areas.

1. As in Figure 5.10, remove the right-hand side of the torso. As mentioned earlier, we will eventually mirror this side of the model to create the other, so there is no need to keep these polygons.

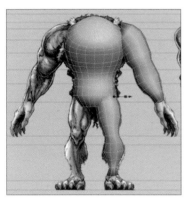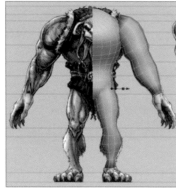

**Figure 5.10** Remove the right-hand side of the torso.

2. Next move in to the pelvis area, as shown in Figure 5.11. Delete the polygons from the lower torso, adjusting them so they roughly match where the leg would naturally join the pelvis.

3. Finally, while we are removing polygons, delete the caps from the cylinders, if those were created initially.

**Figure 5.11** Remove the polygons from the bottom of the torso, adjusting the remaining vertices as shown.

The model is now prepared, so we can easily weld the leg onto the torso.

1. Before you continue you must make sure the three elements are combined into a single object. Most applications will not allow you to weld vertices belonging to two different models.

2. The next step is simply a case of welding/merging the vertices closest to each other as demonstrated in Figure 5.12. You will notice they don't match perfectly, so some vertices will be left, but, not to worry, we can fix this next.

**Figure 5.12** Weld the vertices that are closest to each other.

3. With the main vertices welded you should have two left. What we will do with these is simply delete the edge loop to which they are connected (Figure 5.13).

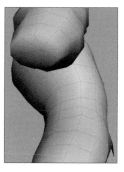

**Figure 5.13** Delete the edge loops of the remaining vertices, smoothing out the area afterward.

4. As you can see, this leaves the side of the torso looking wrong since there is a pinch. Simply slide these edge loops to smooth out the area.

5. The last step to attaching the leg is to fill in the crotch area. Luckily we have an open area that simply needs to be filled, so, as in Figure 5.14, extrude the edges from the leg.

**Figure 5.14** Finally, fill in the hole around the pelvis area.

6. Finally, weld the vertices to the front and back of the crotch area, adjusting the vertices to smooth out the area.

Your Ogre should now look like that in Figure 5.15. All that remains in this stage is to attach the arm.

 Now is a good time to save. For reference you can find the file Ogre_02.obj on the companion CD.

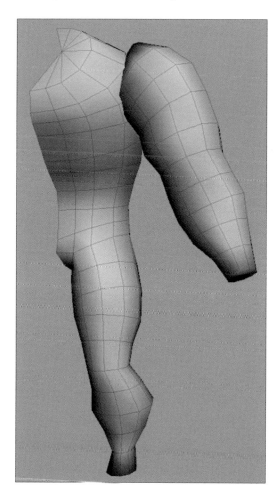

**Figure 5.15**

The leg is attached.

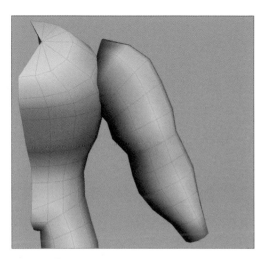 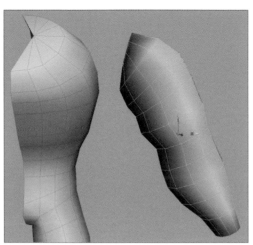 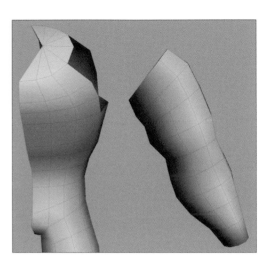

**Figure 5.16** Prepare the area by removing the polygons as shown.

As with the leg, we first need to prepare the area by deleting some of the geometry.

1. Following Figure 5.16, first move the arm away from the torso so you can see the polygons around his shoulder and armpit area.

2. Next, remove the first row of polygons from the arm, and the six quads closest to it from the torso.

3. Looking from above now, bridge the edges around the armpit area, as in Figure 5.17.

4. Continue to bridge the polygons, moving around the shoulder until the hole is filled (Figure 5.18).

5. Finally, move the arm back into position.

The arm and leg are now both happily attached to the torso; your model should now resemble that in Figure 5.19.

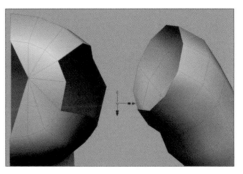

**Figure 5.17**

Bridge the gap starting under the arm.

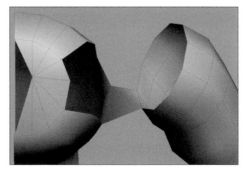

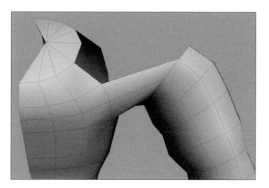 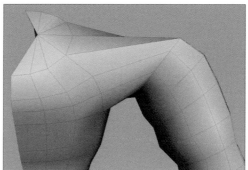 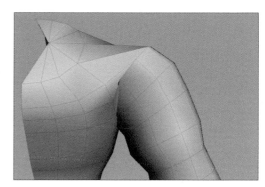

**Figure 5.18**  Work your way around the arm, filling in the gap.

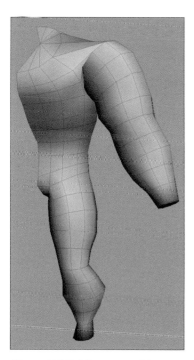 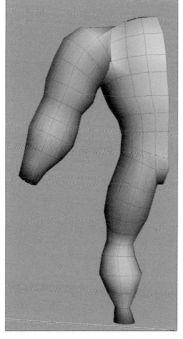

We still have some work to do though. As you can probably tell, the shoulder area doesn't look right. It's all twisted, and areas are overlapping badly. Spend some time now working on the area to tidy it up, but don't worry too much about it being anatomically correct; at this stage we are just looking for a basic shape.

When you're happy with it, remove the polygons at the very top of the torso—the ones where the neck should be. What you may see is an odd-looking polygon, like the one in Figure 5.20.

 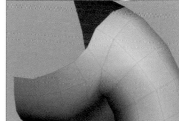

**Figure 5.20**  Remove the top of the torso before fixing the stretched polygon.

**Figure 5.19**  The arm and leg are now attached.

The topology needs to be as smooth as possible, so we need to address this. You can approach it in a few different ways: either remove the geometry and rebuild the area, or split the polygons. Either way you should try and achieve the result in the second pane of Figure 5.20.

All that is left to do now is work your way around the body, smoothing out areas and giving it a general tidy-up until you are happy with it (Figure 5.21).

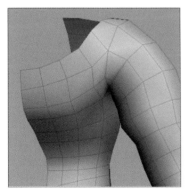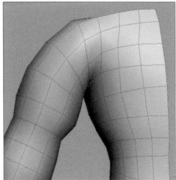

**Figure 5.21**  Tidy up the model before you proceed.

We are off to a good start. We have the basic form of the Ogre created, and the mesh is completely made up of quads.

Now is a good time to save. For reference you can find the file Ogre_03.obj on the companion CD.

# Extremities

Our Ogre has a body but is missing some key elements—namely, his hands, feet and his head. Let's address this, starting with the hands.

## Hands

Hands come in a variety of shapes and sizes, and for a base model, the detail will vary drastically depending on the intentions of the artist. Look at the hand in Figure 5.22. This is very basic, with the fingers simply extruded from the wrist.

**Figure 5.22**

A basic hand model, normally used to sculpt upon.

This type of hand will be used for sculpting. It's clean, and when subdivided will give a nice, predictable topology that will give the artist the optimum start for their sculpture.

For our Ogre we will take a different approach. The model we are creating will eventually become the basis for the in-game character, so we need to add a little more detail.

To begin we will create a finger. By doing this we can then simply copy and scale this finger to act as the rest.

1. Start a new scene and create a cylinder, but this time make sure it has only six divisions around its axis.

2. Take this cylinder and manipulate it until it resembles the Ogre's finger (see Figure 5.23).

**Tip**

If you're struggling, look at your own finger and copy the shape. This character's hands are human shaped, so referring to your own hand will give you a good start.

 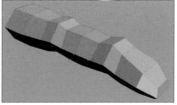

**Figure 5.23** Create a basic cylinder and manipulate it to match the Ogre's finger.

3. Our Ogre has long finger nails, more like claws really, so let's add these into the model. Following Figure 5.24, first duplicate the polygons at the finger's end and scale them inward.

4. Finally, add another extrusion, pulling out the geometry that will act as the finger nail.

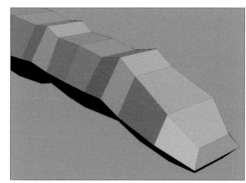

**Figure 5.24**

Extrude polygons at the end of the finger to act as the nail.

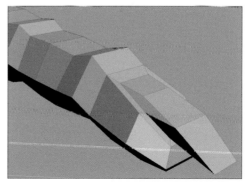

That's the main finger complete; we can now use this to generate the rest. As demonstrated in Figure 5.25, duplicate the finger four times and reposition them to act as the remaining fingers and thumb.

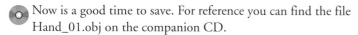 Now is a good time to save. For reference you can find the file Hand_01.obj on the companion CD.

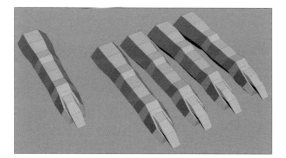

**Figure 5.25**

Duplicate your finger four times and position them to act as the remaining fingers and thumb.

**Note**

As you will notice, each finger not only differs in size but also orientation. Examine your own hand and you will see that each finger tilts slightly as you move down the hand.

Notice that fingers don't start, or lie, on the same plane. Starting from the ring finger, the index and middle fingers are set back slightly, while the little finger originates even farther back.

Now we need to connect our fingers.

1. Looking from behind the fingers, start to bridge the gaps between them. For now, just add two polygons between each (see Figure 5.26).

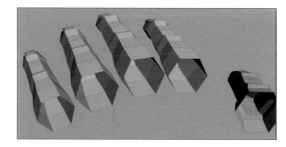

**Figure 5.26**

Start to bridge the gaps between each finger.

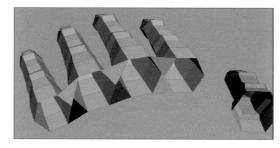

2. Now select the edge loop behind the fingers and extrude the polygons backward until they are just past the thumb.

3. Finally, as shown in Figure 5.27, create two splits across the new geometry. Make sure these splits follow the hand all the way around.

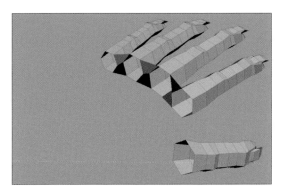

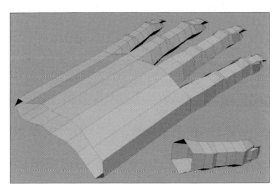

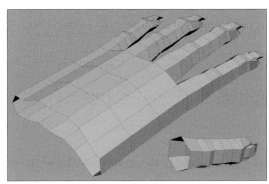

**Figure 5.27**

Extrude the polygons back behind the fingers and divide that new space twice.

Now let's connect the thumb.

1. Following Figure 5.28, first delete the four polygons from the side of the hand—those closest to the thumb.

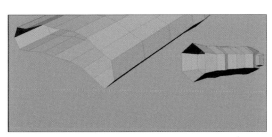

**Figure 5.28**

Now connect the thumb to the hand.

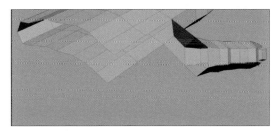

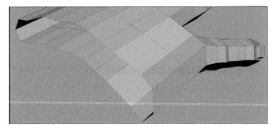

2. Next add two polygons, connecting the side of the thumb to the hand.

3. Finally, extrude the polygons back behind the thumb, making sure to weld the vertices.

That's the main section of the hand completed. There is still work to be done though; as you can see from Figure 5.29, the shape of the hand is wrong.

Take some time now to work on the overall shape of the hand. Don't go too far though, as we aren't looking for a perfect model at this stage. Remember, we are only building the foundations with this model. You should aim to create something like the hand in Figure 5.30.

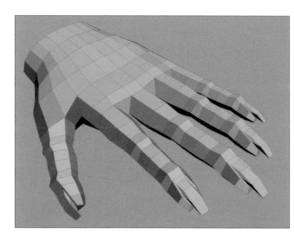

**Figure 5.30**

Rework the hand until you have a shape similar to this.

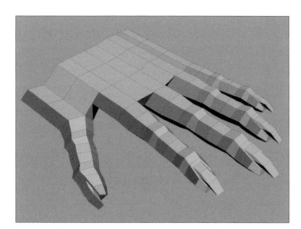

**Figure 5.29**

The hand still needs work.

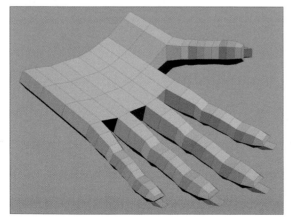

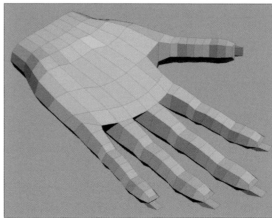

Our hand is now complete, so save the model so you can import it into the same scene as our torso and limbs and attach it to the arm.

Now is a good time to save. For reference you can find the file Hand_02.obj on the companion CD.

1. Import the Ogre base mesh into the hand scene and, using the model sheet as a guide, rotate and scale the hand not only to match the concept but also to line up with the wrist (see Figure 5.31).

2. As demonstrated in Figure 5.32, weld every second vertex to the corresponding one on the wrist. You may not have exactly double the amount of vertices on the hand as you do on the wrist, but don't worry, make sure these are still welded but on the inner wrist.

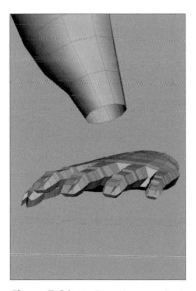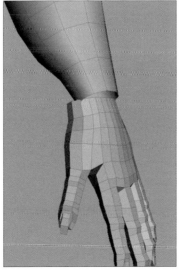

**Figure 5.31** Scale and rotate the hand to line up with the wrist.

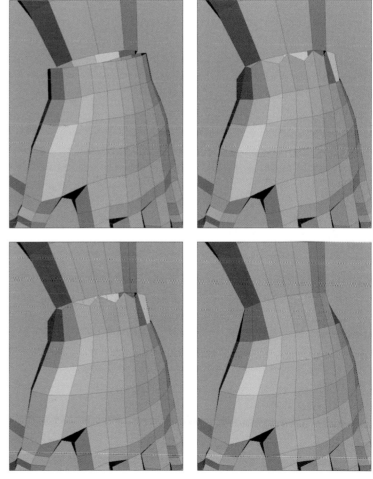

**Figure 5.32** Attach the hand to the wrist.

3. To help finish the stitching, divide the polygons on the wrist. This will create extra vertices to weld to.

At this stage we could leave the hand as is, although a little work on the vertices would help to refine the shape of the wrist and smooth out the area. One thing we could address are the new splits we added into the wrist. Adding these has turned the quads above them into five-sided polygons, but this isn't necessarily a problem; these will give a usable division, but ideally we want them to remain quads.

1. Select each edge ring that flows between each knuckle. Make sure the correct edges are selected on the palm of the hand.

2. Collapsing these will bring us closer to our goal (see Figure 5.33). Yes, we lose the polygons between each finger, but this is an early stage in the character-building process, so if we need them we can add them back into our actual game model.

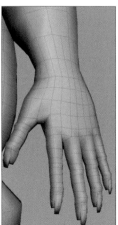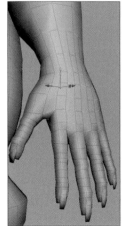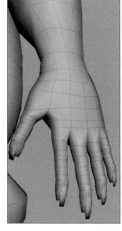

**Figure 5.33** Collapsing the edges flowing back from between the fingers will return our quads.

3. You will notice that we still have some redundant splits in the sides of our wrist (see Figure 5.34). To remove these we can alter the flow of the quads, in effect turning it back toward the hand. First delete the two higher, vertical splits.

4. Next split the polygons beneath these two.

5. Finally weld the vertices above to the ones to their left and right sides. As you can see, this gives us back our quads by simply redirecting the loop. In addition, the location of this loop will be hidden as it will act as detail for the wrist.

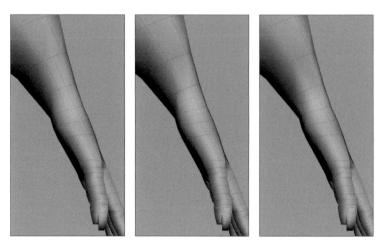

**Figure 5.34** Redirect the polygon flow to help us remove the five-sided polygons (*n*-gons).

6. That's one side done, but looking at the other side (see Figure 5.35), we have a slightly different problem. Here we have just one split, but we also have a triangle.

7. Again, redirecting the flow of the polygon loops will help us eliminate both these problems. Following Figure 5.35, create a horizontal split from the triangle across to the split causing the *n*-gon.

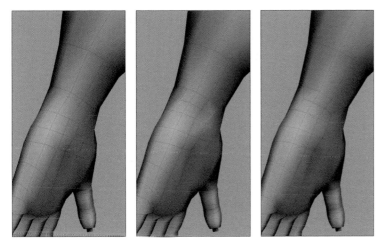

**Figure 5.35** Redirect the polygon loop to help remove the *n*-gon and triangle.

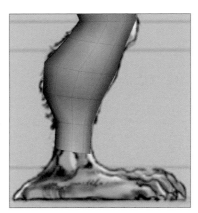

**Figure 5.36**

Extrude the edges, and then the faces, to create the basic shape of the foot.

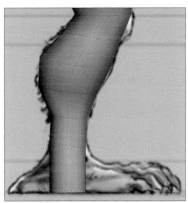

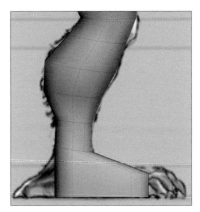

8. As you did before, weld the upper vertex to the one to its left.

9. Finally, move the new vertex in the triangle to give us a nicely quaded area.

That's the hands added, and in addition we have explored some problem areas that arise when generating a quad-based model. Next we will create his feet.

# Feet

Compared to the hands, the creation of the feet on our character should be an easier task. In this case we won't need to drop into a new file; instead we will create them already attached to the leg.

1. Following Figure 5.36, switch to the side view and focus on the base of the leg.

2. Extrude the edges down to the base of the feet.

3. Next select the front five faces from the new geometry and extrude them out in front of the leg. We need to select five faces so we have one for each toe.

4. Move to the front view now and edit the shape of the foot, pulling the vertices out to match the foot in the model sheet (see Figure 5.37).

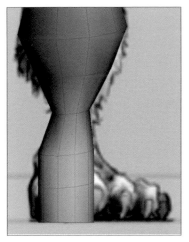 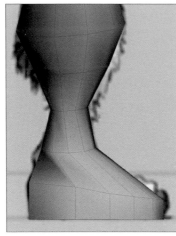

**Figure 5.37** Work on the foot shape, filling it out from the front view.

That's the main bulk of the foot created; now let's look at the toes.

1. We already have the base for each toe, so extrude the polygons from the front of the foot, making sure they remain separate (see Figure 5.38).

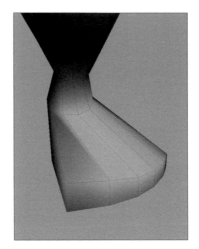 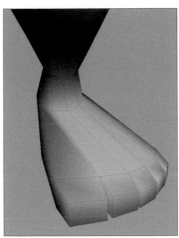

**Figure 5.38** Extrude the polygons at the front of the foot to create the toes.

2. Time to add some detail. Following Figure 5.39, create a split across the main area of the foot, across the toes, and around the whole foot.

3. With these new vertices at your disposal, go ahead and rework the overall shape of the foot.

With the hand we created finger nails to add a bit of detail to the model. Looking at our concept we can see that the Ogre has claws that come out of the front of his toes. We will need to model these into the base mesh so we can paint detail into them later.

1. As demonstrated in Figure 5.40, extrude the polygons at the front of each toe, but instead of pulling these out, simply scale them inward.

2. Next, create another extrude, but this time pull the faces out to create the claws.

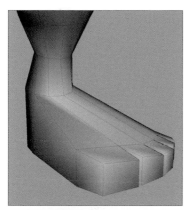

**Figure 5.39**

Add more divisions so you can work more detail into the shape of the foot.

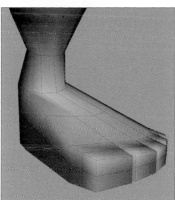

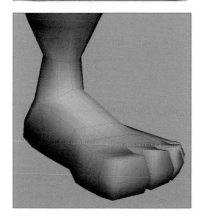

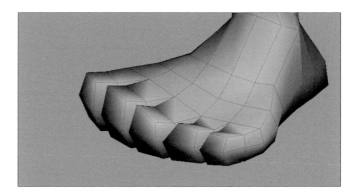

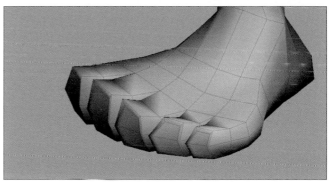

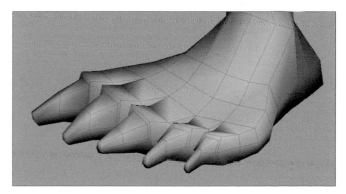

**Figure 5.40** Extrude the polygons at the front of the foot to create the toes.

3. Finally, add another split, dividing the claws so we can create a slight curve.

4. There is one more claw to create, so move to the back of the foot.

5. Again, create an initial extrude on the rear polygon, scaling it inward.

6. Pull the faces back out and create the shape of the claw, like in Figure 5.41.

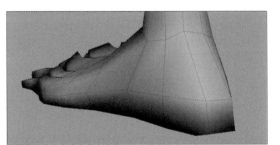

**Figure 5.41**

Now create a claw at the back of the foot.

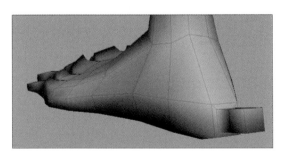

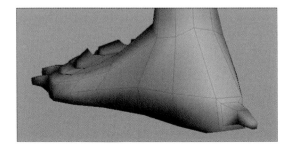

There we have it. Our creature is starting to take shape. At this stage you can duplicate and mirror the model like in Figure 5.42, so you can get a better feeling for how the character is shaping up.

Now is a good time to save. For reference you can find the file Ogre_04.obj on the companion CD.

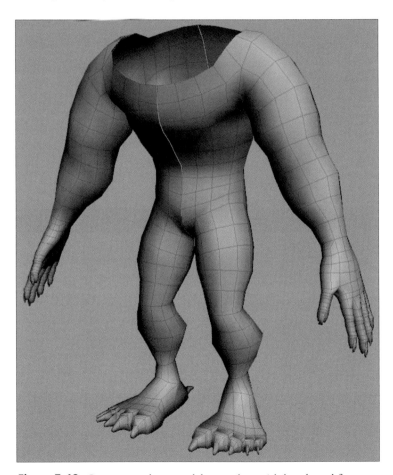

**Figure 5.42** Our current base model, complete with hands and feet.

# Head and Face

The head of any character is a major part; it's the element looked upon the most, so it has to portray a convincing likeness of the character. In this section we will construct the Ogre's head, but it's important to note that we are not concerned with it being exact at this stage. What we will need is good topology not only for sculpting upon but also for deformation. You see, to make a face move realistically it's important that the position of edge loops follow the actual facial muscle structure.

Normally this would be left until the construction of the actual game model, but we are aiming to use this model, with some optimizations, as our real-time model.

We will cover this further throughout the section.

> **Note**
>
> For the head I will be adopting Silo's Symmetry Mode, which will take any actions I perform on one side and apply it to the other. If your application of choice doesn't have a similar tool, simply work on one side of the head, as we did with the body; you can always mirror it later, or simply use a mirrored instance.

## The Basic Shape

First, as with any model, we need to block out the basic shape, but this time we are going to start with a cube.

1. As illustrated in Figure 5.43, create a cube and add three divisions both horizontally and vertically, with just one division down the side.

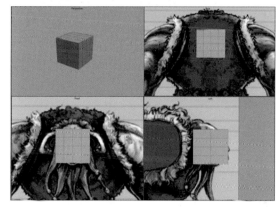

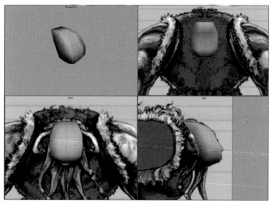

**Figure 5.43**

We begin the head with a simple cube. After subdividing it, adjust the shape.

2. With the extra detail added, adjust the overall shape to fit the basic shape of the head in the model sheet.

3. Next work the overall shape a bit further, trying to define the eyes and nose (see Figure 5.44).

4. Finally, add more divisions, using the new vertices to define more areas of the face (see Figure 5.45).

That's the basic head. Granted, it is very basic, but bear with me.

## Eyes

Your eyelids lay over your eyeball, following the curve of its surface. This shape is sometimes difficult to achieve with no actual eyeball in your model. Before we begin to work on the surrounding eye area, it's a good idea to have some mock eyeballs in place for you to work around.

Using the model sheet as a guide, place two spheres into the scene and position them where the eyes would be. Don't worry if, like in Figure 5.46, this looks strange, since it shows just how far off we were with our original estimate.

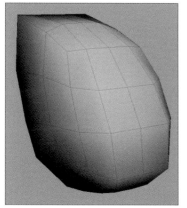

**Figure 5.44** Work the model further to closer match the shape of the head.

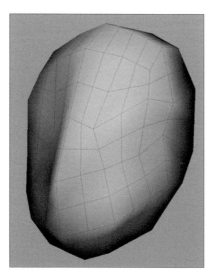
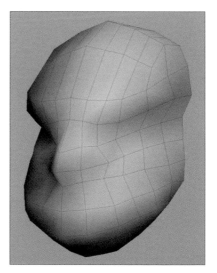

**Figure 5.45**

Add more divisions to the model before adding more detail to the shape.

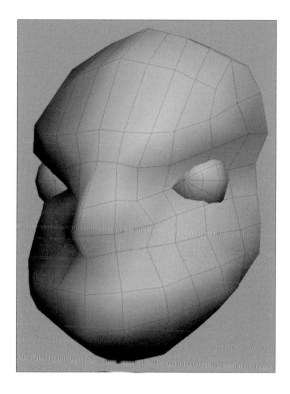

**Figure 5.46**

Place two spheres into the scene to act as mock eyeballs.

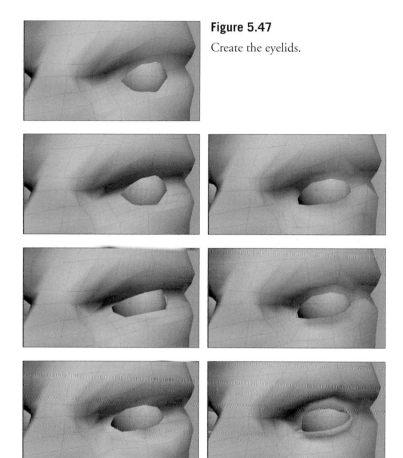

**Figure 5.47**

Create the eyelids.

Now, with the eyeballs in place, let's start to build the actual eyelids.

1. Following Figure 5.47, first divide the polygons around the eye area. Do this both horizontally and vertically.

2. There should be a clear section of polygons covering the actual eyeball. Delete these to create an opening for the eye.

3. Manipulate the vertices to create a more natural shape around the eye.

4. Now is the tricky part: We need to rebuild some of the eye so we have nice, clean loops. As mentioned at the start of this section, these loops will follow the muscles of the eye, helping it to look and deform correctly. So, using what you have already learned in this section, collapse edges at the corners of the eye until the polygons flow nicely around the opening.

5. With the main loop in place we can now add more detail, first splitting our initial loop before moving out from the eye to create more loops.

6. Finally, adjust the new vertices to create eyelids.

Now, switching to the front, we can see our eyes are too large (see Figure 5.48). Take some time now to work on the eyes until they resemble the Ogre's, also making sure you try your best to eliminate any triangles that may have appeared.

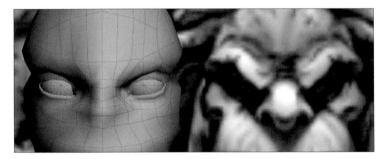

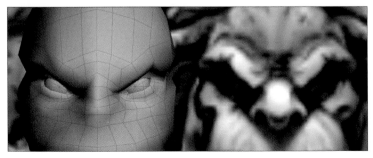

**Figure 5.48** Adjust the eyes and brow to match the head in the model sheet.

The actual image plane may be too low resolution to work from at this point, so refer to the higher-resolution model sheet found on the companion CD to help you.

## Mouth

The mouth should be an easier shape to model.

1. First we need more detail in the mouth area, so create two horizontal divisions, as shown in Figure 5.49.

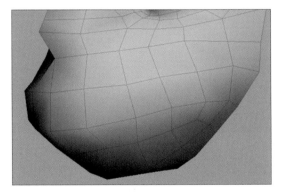

**Figure 5.49**

Create two horizontal divisions across the mouth.

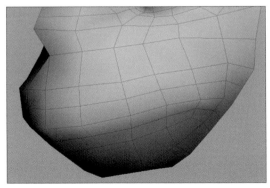

2. Next, switch to the side view and work on the mouth to achieve the correct shape (see Figure 5.50).

**Figure 5.50** From the side, adjust the new vertices to match the mouth shape.

The problem we have at this point is that the mouth wraps around the head with no beginning or end. What we will do next is build in the corners of the mouth and, while doing so, add crucial edge loops into the topology, again to match real-life muscles.

1. Following Figure 5.51, first create two cuts where the corner of the mouth will be.

2. From the new cuts, create four more as illustrated in Figure 5.51.

**Figure 5.51**
Create the corner of the mouth, making sure to retain the edge loops.

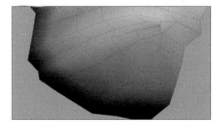

3. Now we can safely remove two edges, giving us a nice loop around the mouth.

4. There is, however, a triangle above and below the corner of the mouth. We can easily remove these by collapsing the edges that move back from them and to the edge of the head.

To complete the mouth, we need to open it slightly, but in doing this, we will inevitably create a new triangle. To fix this, we can simply follow the opening around the head, cutting the polygons before moving the vertices to smooth out the area. You can see this demonstrated in Figure 5.52.

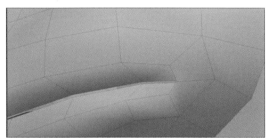

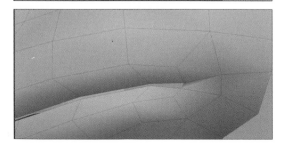

**Figure 5.52**

Follow the cut around the head to remove unwanted triangles.

That's the outer mouth complete, for now. Usually for a game model the inner mouth will also be needed. This would include teeth, a tongue, and the actual inner walls. For this example piece we will skip these features, as I am sure you are capable of modeling these without direction.

## Nose

With the eyes and mouth created, all that is left to do is add his nose.

1. Following Figure 5.53, begin by adding some divisions across the face so you can add more detail into the nose.

2. Move into the nose area now. You should have a collection of four polygons roughly where the nostrils are. Select these and extrude them inward to create the cavity (see Figure 5.54).

3. Now we need to add more detail to smooth the nostril, but we don't want any more divisions across the head as this will create lots of unneeded polygons. Instead, we'll add an edge loop that will move around the opening. As illustrated in Figure 5.55, start by cutting just the top, bottom, left, and right polygons just outside the nostril.

4. Now connect these new cuts, creating triangles at each corner.

5. Collapsing these edges will not only remove the triangles but will also complete the loop.

6. To finish, work on the area to refine the nose's shape until you end up with something resembling Figure 5.56.

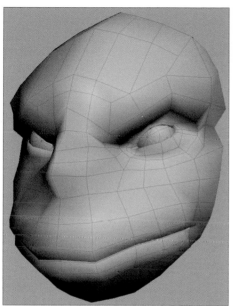

**Figure 5.53**

Divide the face so you can add more detail in the nose area.

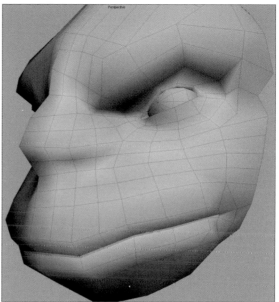

**Figure 5.54**

Extrude the polygons to create the nostril cavity.

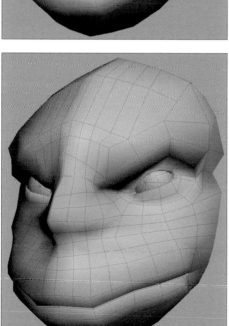

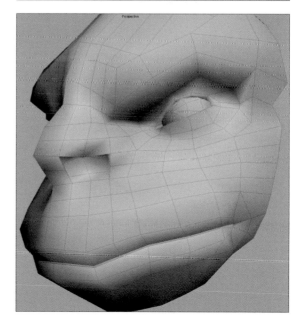

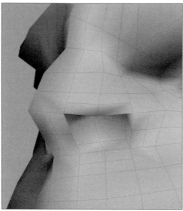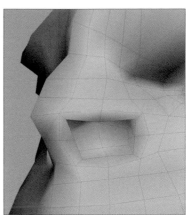

**Figure 5.55** Split the polygons to create a new edge loop around his nostril.

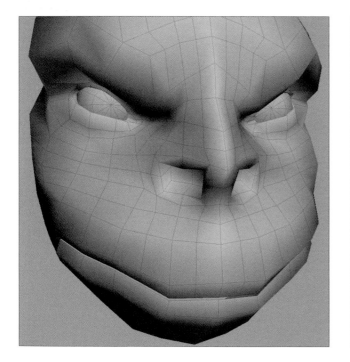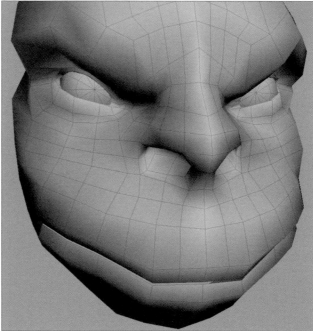

**Figure 5.56**

With the extra geometry added, refine the nose area.

The nose is OK as it stands, but what we want ideally is the crease behind the nostrils to be defined a little more. To do this we need to add another edge loop.

1. As you did with the nostril, split the polygons across the bridge of the nose, beneath the nose and the side of the nostril (see Figure 5.57).

2. Next connect the polygons, creating triangles at each corner.

3. Finally collapse the corner edges, creating the loop.

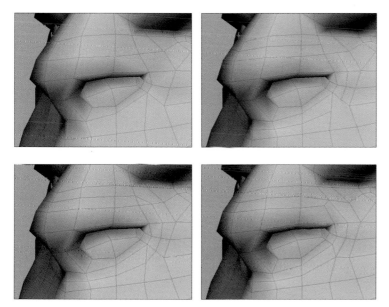

**Figure 5.57** Add a further edge loop to help define the nostril.

If you like, you can use this opportunity to work further on the nose, but don't feel like you need to. We will add most of the detail later, in Chapter 7. Before moving on to the ears though, spend some time tweaking the head and fixing any minor problems with its topology. For example, next to the eyes we have a five-sided polygon. This isn't a major problem, but the way it's formed may cause issues later.

This can be fixed easily in two steps.

1. As shown in Figure 5.58, first create a split that runs under the head and up to the side of the eye.

2. Weld the two vertices near the top of the split, turning the *n*-gon into a quad.

So that's the base mesh for the main head, but before you attach it to the body, you need to create the Ogre's large ears.

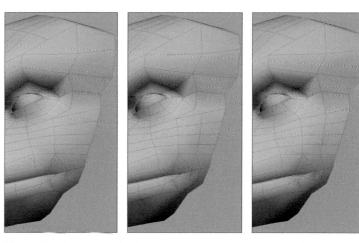

**Figure 5.58** Create a further split to help remove the *n*-gon beside the eye.

# Ears

The final part of our creature is his ears. They aren't simple shapes hidden by his hair; these are monsters in themselves and therefore need to be created correctly so we can add the right amount of detail.

1. As is Figure 5.59, switch to the front view and extrude the edges at the back of the head horizontally to form the front of the ears.

2. Divide the ears three times, so you have nice quads to work with and not long strips.

3. Now adjust the new geometry to a rough ear shape.

4. We next need to give thickness to the ear, so switch to a perspective view, similar to that in Figure 5.60, and extrude the back of the head, including the edges around the ears.

5. Now we need to provide a back to the ears. You can approach this however you like, but for this exercise you could simply copy the polygons from the front and weld them to create the rear (see Figure 5.61).

6. All that is left to do now is adjust the general shape of the ears until you are happy. You can see an example in Figure 5.62.

**Figure 5.59**

Extrude the polygons out to the sides of his head to create the foundations for the ears.

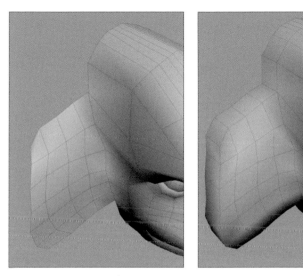

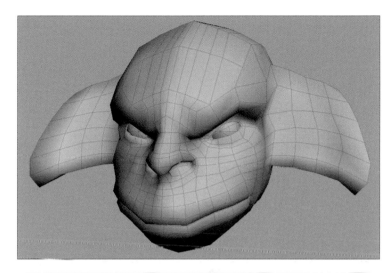

**Figure 5.60** Extrude the edges at the back of the head to give thickness to the ears.

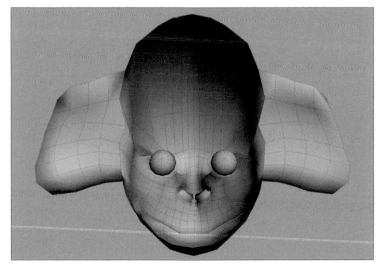

**Figure 5.61** Create a back for the ears.

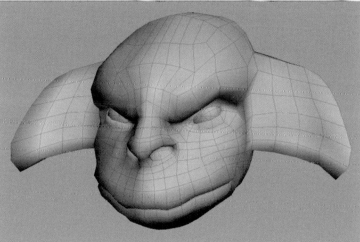

**Figure 5.62** Adjust the ears and the overall shape of the head until you are happy.

The head is now complete, and you should now have something similar to that in Figure 5.63. To finish the main body, all you need to do is attach the head to the torso.

Now is a good time to save. For reference you can find the file Ogre_05.obj on the companion CD.

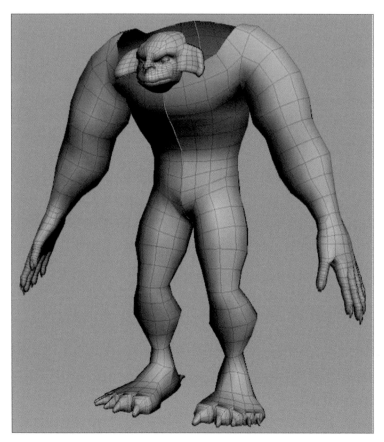

**Figure 5.63** The complete base head and body.

## Attaching the Head

Connecting the head to the torso may seem like a simple task. All we need to do is weld the vertices, create bridges, and extrude a few edges, right? Well, not exactly. Our head has more divisions than the torso, so we can't do a straight connect without creating creases or triangles. What we need to do is reroute some of the edge loops back into the head, which will reduce or even eliminate any triangles in our model.

### Note

I must stress that this is just one way of doing this. Please feel free to follow your own path if you wish.

To make things easier, first remove half of the head and body, just leaving the Ogre's left side, as shown in Figure 5.64.

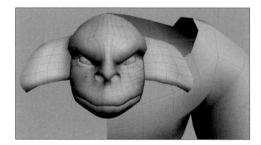

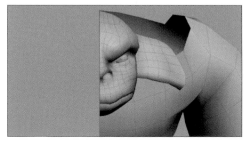

**Figure 5.64**

Remove the right side of the Ogre's head and body to make things a little easier.

1. Now, following Figure 5.65, begin to bridge the gap between the head and torso, starting at the top.

2. Create two divisions across the new polygons so you can continue to add geometry across to the shoulder.

3. Next collapse the two triangles to remove them and join the surrounding quads.

There remains an obvious *n*-gon on the top of the Ogre's head, but you can leave this for now and move down to under the Ogre's chin.

This area needs to be tweaked, pulling the vertices down so the polygons run under the head (see Figure 5.66).

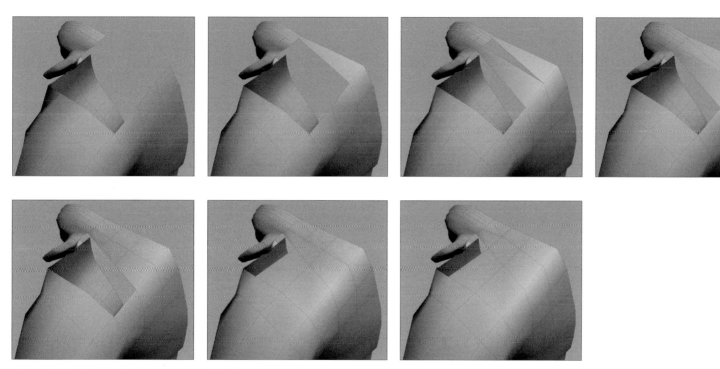

**Figure 5.65** Start at the top of the head, bridging the gap between the head and torso.

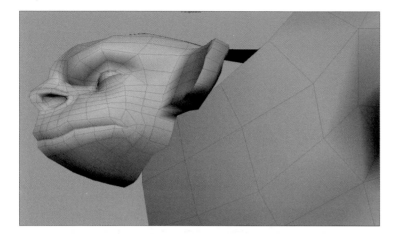

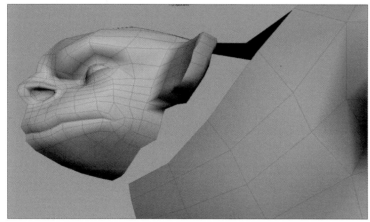

**Figure 5.66** Manipulate the vertices around the neck.

With the shape adjusted you can continue the stitching.

1. Select the edges running under the chin, following them all the way up above the ear.

2. Extrude these edges to create new polygons, pulling them back to line up with the edge above the head while making sure to weld the vertices (see Figure 5.67).

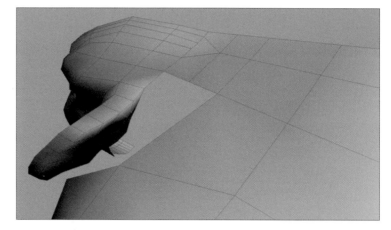

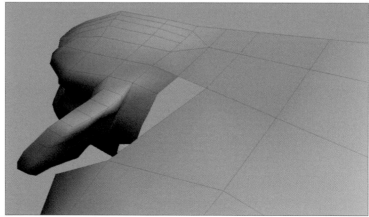

**Figure 5.67** Extrude the remaining edges back to create depth for the Ogre's neck.

Now that we have this extra geometry, we can continue to fill in the gap. Move back to the upper shoulder and bridge the hole as shown in Figure 5.68, connecting the new polygons with those on the shoulder.

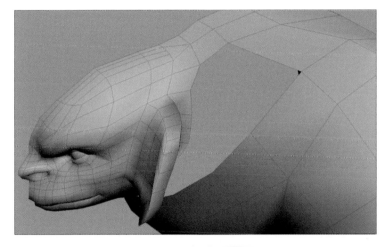

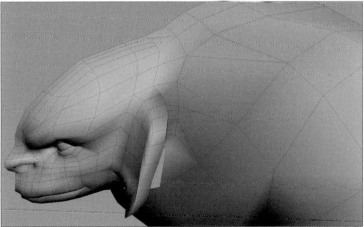

**Figure 5.68** Connect the new polygons to those on the shoulder.

Moving back down, now you can see in Figure 5.69 that the Ogre's chin has quite a few divisions; in fact it has five more than the polygon below it on the chest. We will have to adjust the chest so we can successfully connect the two.

1. Following Figure 5.69, split the first four polygons down the chest, adding a further vertical split across the lower polygon.

2. As you did earlier, weld the open vertex to the one on its right to complete the edge loop.

3. Now move onto the head, merging the four vertices under the chin (see Figure 5.70).

4. Next weld the three lower vertices to those closest to them on the torso.

5. Now you can work on the side of the head. Again we have more vertices on the head, so select all the open vertices and weld them.

6. To fill the final hole, simply take this single vertex and weld it to the one across from it (see Figure 5.71).

This will look a little messy, but we will tidy it up later. The important thing is that the head is now fully connected. Let's move on and address the triangles, and the ugly areas.

1. Looking from above, we have a few triangles, as you can see in Figure 5.72. To help us later, we will need to create a split through these.

2. Next collapse the edges down the center of each triangle. This action doesn't remove the triangles, it just moves them, but the extra division will be useful.

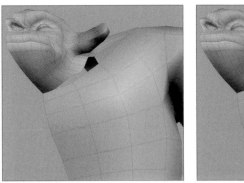
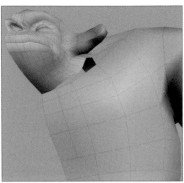
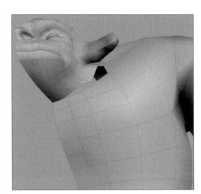
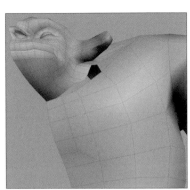

**Figure 5.69**  Create a split in the chest.

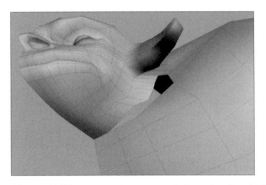
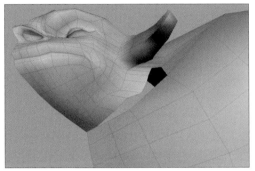
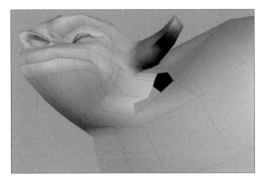

**Figure 5.70**  Merge the vertices below the chin before welding them to the torso.

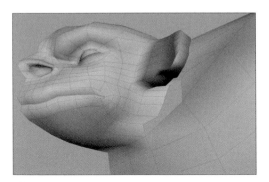
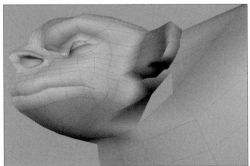
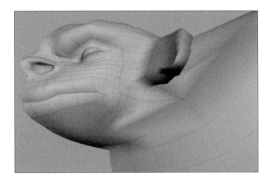

**Figure 5.71**  Weld the vertices around the final hole to fill it.

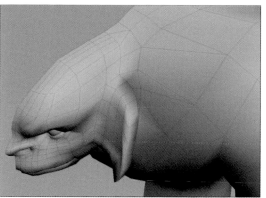

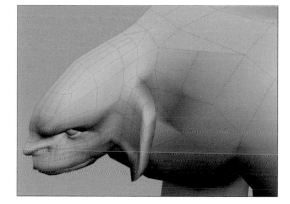

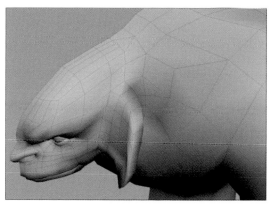

**Figure 5.72**

Cut the triangles to the side of the head.

3. Move to beneath the head now so we can address the problems in this area.

4. Following Figure 5.73, first collapse the two outer triangles under the neck.

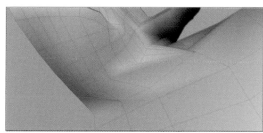

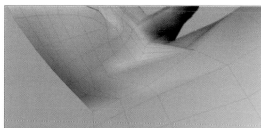

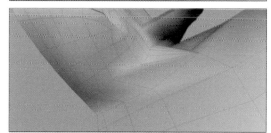

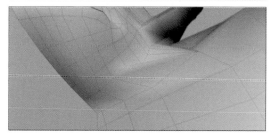

**Figure 5.73**

Collapse the two triangles under the neck and add a split to define the edge loop.

5. Next create a split running from the first triangle down through the three quads below it, making sure to adjust the split so it ends in quads.

6. Moving back up to the first triangle closest to the middle of the Ogre, use a similar method to change this into quads (Figure 5.74).

7. Finally move around the neck and split the quad shown in Figure 5.74, deleting the edge that made up the triangle. This does create a new triangle, but what you've done is opened up the flow of quads from the chest up onto the head.

As you can see, this can be a complicated task. Trust me, it's difficult enough to try and record it, but bear with me. As mentioned earlier, feel free to use your own method; this section is merely a guide that I am using to demonstrate how to remove triangles and reroute edge loops.

Let's continue.

1. Now, following Figure 5.75, create a split down the neck and onto the torso.

2. Add another cut, this time running back from the first split and up to the cut you added earlier.

3. Collapsing the first edge will remove the triangle and also reroute the quads; the problem now is that we have an *n*-gon.

4. Creating a cut as demonstrated in Figure 5.75 will help remove this, as collapsing the triangle will bring the quads back.

5. Finally, tidy up the area, smoothing out the topology.

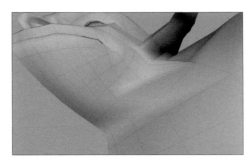

**Figure 5.74**

Convert the first triangle into quads before dividing the quad around the neck.

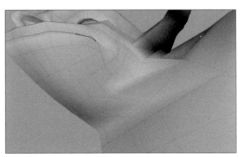

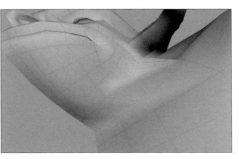

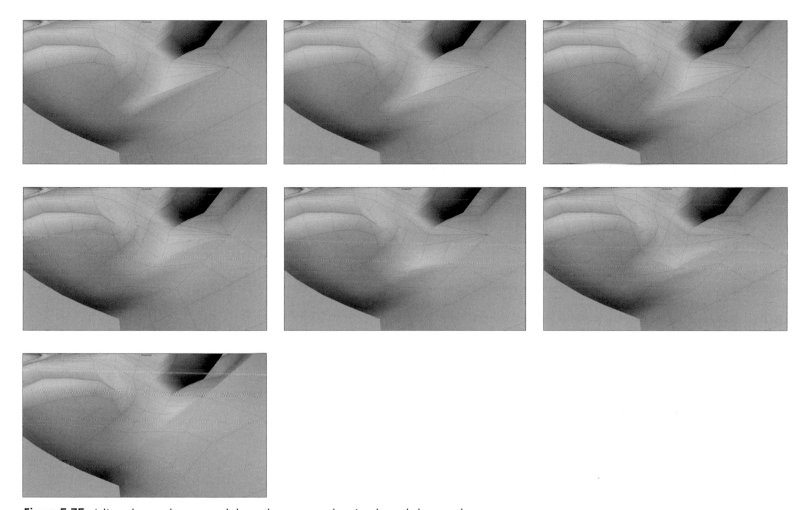

**Figure 5.75** Adjust the topology around the neck to remove the triangles and clean up the area.

I hope that you are starting to see how you can remove triangles and affect the flow of edge loops to achieve better topology and form.

1. Pull back slightly to reveal more of the shoulder, as in Figure 5.76.

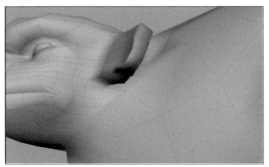

**Figure 5.76**

Create a cut from the neck to the shoulder.

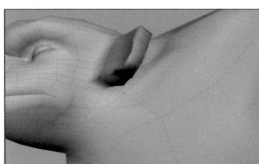

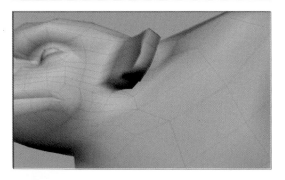

2. Create a cut flowing from the neck and up onto the Ogre's shoulder, but not over it.

3. Collapse the edge between the triangle and the *n*-gon, turning it into a quad.

We now have a weird-shaped *n*-gon behind the ear; you can see this in Figure 5.77. This time we won't collapse one of its edges; instead we will divide it to help us with the top of the head. This is shown in Figure 5.77.

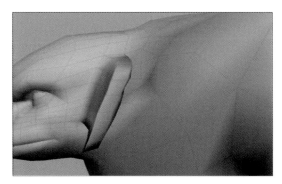

**Figure 5.77**

Alter the *n*-gon by adding a split through it, following it onto the shoulder.

Looking at Figure 5.78, we could simply collapse the lower and upper edges of the two triangles, removing them from the model. Instead we are going to take a different approach so we can introduce another edge loop.

1. Following Figure 5.78, flip the edges of the triangles until you have a similar result.

2. Moving back to the top of his shoulders, create a cut running back from where his head joined his torso. You can see this in Figure 5.79.

3. Next divide the triangle and remove the edge crossing the quad.

4. Now collapse the smaller triangle. This will remove it but will also create a new one, which we will work on next.

5. Continuing in Figure 5.79, split the four quads above the triangle and the two larger ones next to it.

6. Collapse your final cut to remove the triangle before selecting and collapsing the ring of edges running back from the new triangle.

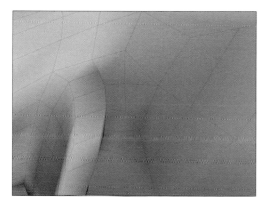 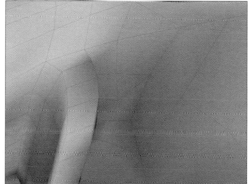 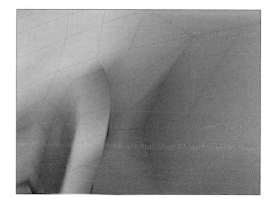

**Figure 5.78** Flip the edges of the triangles.

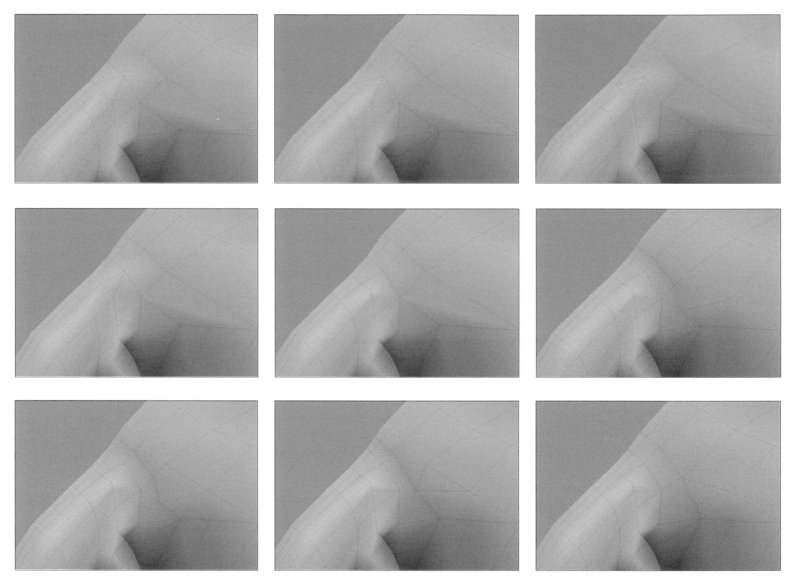

**Figure 5.79** Rework the topology across the shoulders.

We are almost done; we just have a few more steps to go.

1. As illustrated in Figure 5.80, create a cut that will join our earlier division to the shoulders.

2. Collapse this new cut to delete the triangle.

3. We still have two triangles glaring at us, but we can remove these easily. Simply add a cut between the two, collapsing it to convert them into quads.

We are on to our final area, and it's time to remove the triangle on the top of the head.

1. Add a division that runs across the triangle, connecting with the open edge next to it (Figure 5.81).

2. Collapse the smaller triangle and then the ring of edges running from the one above.

3. Now work on the area, smoothing out the quads and refining the form.

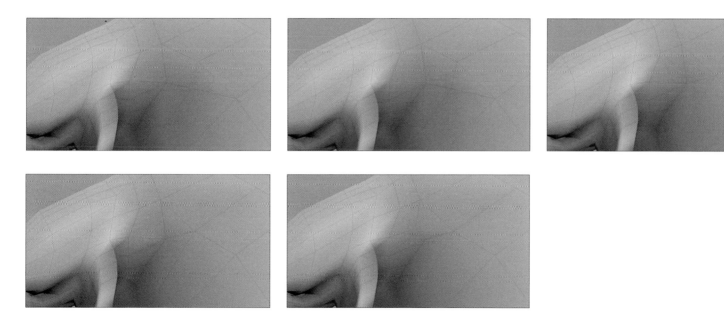

**Figure 5.80** Connect your earlier cut to the shoulder and remove the unwanted triangles.

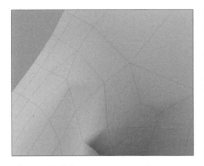
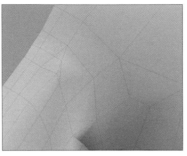
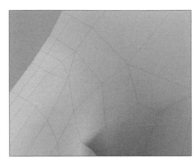
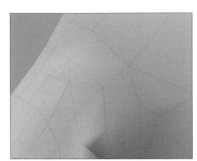

**Figure 5.81** Remove the final triangle and smooth out the area.

Now take a break and look at what you have achieved. Figure 5.82 shows our connected head and torso, free from triangles, but what it also shows is the smoothed version of our creature.

This smoothed version gives us a good idea of the flow of polygons, and how the surface will look when subdivided. As you can see, it flows nicely with no creases or pinches.

The main body of our Ogre is complete. At this stage you could mirror the geometry to get a fuller picture of your character, like in Figure 5.83.

Now is a good time to save. For reference you can find the file Ogre_06.obj on the companion CD.

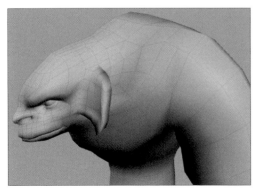
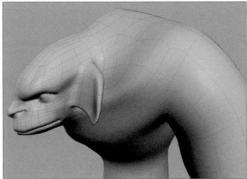
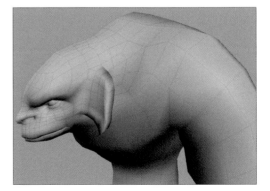

**Figure 5.82** The head is now connected and works well when subdivided.

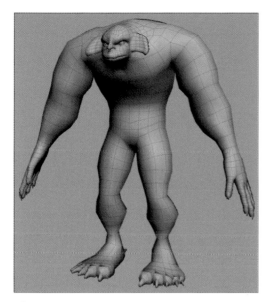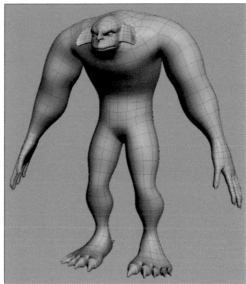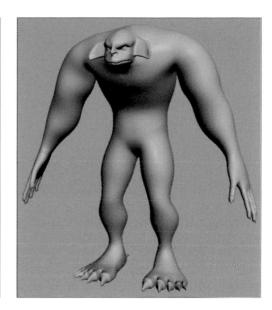

**Figure 5.83** The completed Ogre, normal and subdivided.

# Hair and Fur

Both hair and fur can be a nightmare to create for a real-time model, and this creature has plenty of both. For now, though, you don't need to worry. The fur on his calves, head, and around the top of his sleeves can be added toward the end of the project, so for now let's look at adding his beard.

For the base mesh we aren't looking for anything complicated; just some simple shapes will work for now.

1. As in Figure 5.84, look from under the chin and extrude the six central polygons.

2. Repeat this procedure, extruding three polygons from either side.

3. Move to the front now and extrude more polygons just in front of the ear (see Figure 5.85).

4. Extrude these further, pulling them down and adding a further division.

5. Finally, switch to the front and extend the middle three extrusions. As you can see in Figure 5.86, they don't need to be perfectly shaped; in fact, leaving them separated like this will help when we come to sculpting in the detail.

That's the basic beard created, so now let's look at his clothing.

Now is a good time to save. For reference you can find the file Ogre_07.obj on the companion CD.

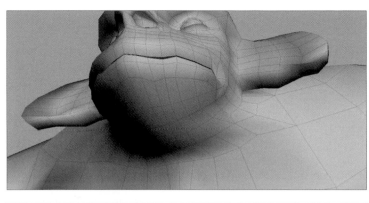

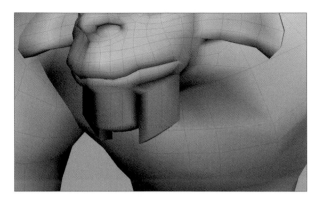

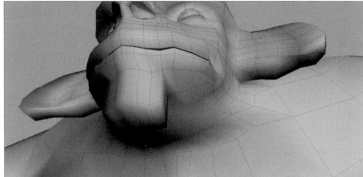

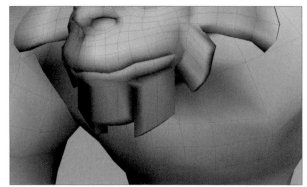

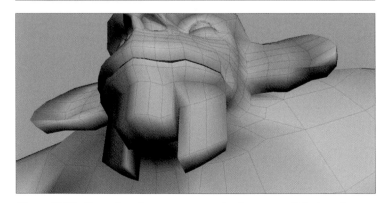

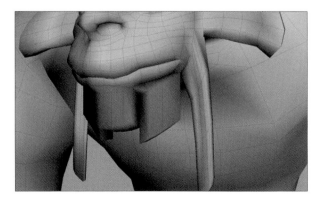

**Figure 5.84** Extrude polygons to create the first parts of the beard.

**Figure 5.85** Extrude polygons in front of the ear, extending them to create the basic beard shape.

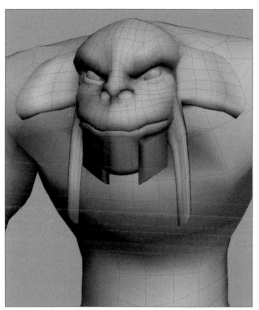

**Figure 5.86**
Extend the middle three extrusions to complete the basic beard.

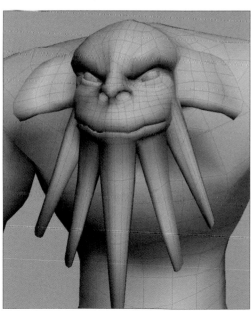

# Clothing

With the body complete we can now move on to his clothing. As with any model, this can be approached in many ways. You could leave the Ogre as is and sculpt the shirt detail directly onto this model. In my experience this can cause problems, so I like to take another approach.

## Shirt

To create the base shirt model, let's generate a separate piece of geometry. We will do this for a number of reasons. First, using a separate model will make sculpting easier, and quicker. Second, this will help to bring the shirt to life as it won't be seamlessly welded to the arms, and, finally, it will help when we come to apply UV data and ultimately texture the beast.

1. Looking at Figure 5.87, we will work with just half of the model. Select the polygons that roughly cover the shirt area and duplicate them, making sure they are a separate element.

2. Our new model's topology now needs work, so remove some of the redundant edges and simplify the shape until you have something resembling Figure 5.88.

3. Bring back the main model and you will see that some of the polygons are intersecting with the Ogre's torso (Figure 5.89). To complete the shirt, simply pull the vertices so the shirt lies outside the Ogre's body.

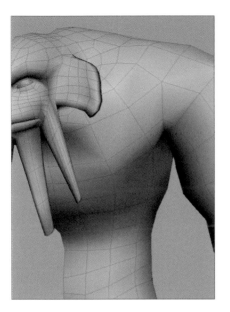

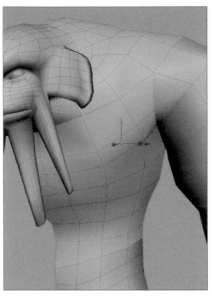

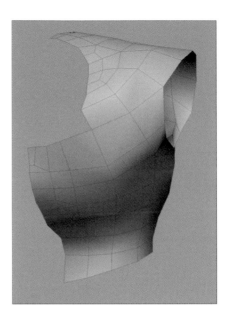

**Figure 5.87**
Duplicate the polygons that cover the general shirt area.

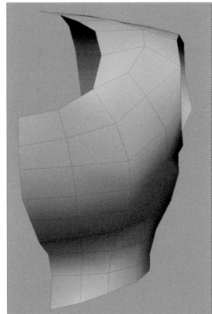

**Figure 5.88**
Adjust the shirts topology to clean it up.

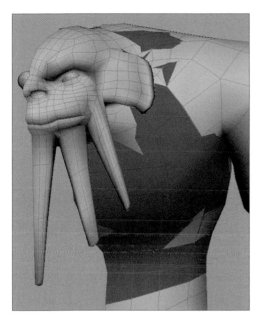

**Figure 5.89**

Pull the vertices of the shirt out so they lie outside the base Ogre mesh.

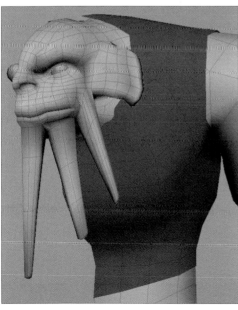

# Loin Cloth

There is no other way to approach the loin cloth than to generate a separate model. Rather than just having a cylinder wrap around his waist, we will add the actual folds into the model.

1. As illustrated in Figure 5.90, begin with a flat plane.

2. Add two divisions and pull the center out.

3. Create two more divisions and adjust the shape to more of a horseshoe shape.

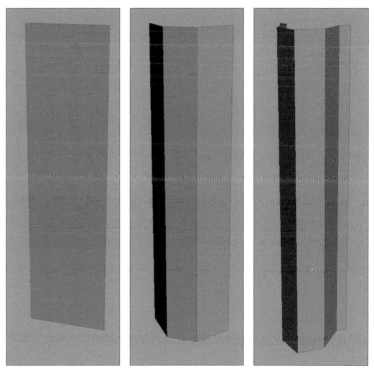

**Figure 5.90** First create a single fold of the cloth.

4. Bring back the main model and position the fold in front of his waist.

5. Duplicate the fold, positioning the copies around his waist; you can see this in Figure 5.91.

Now you have the basic loin cloth shape, and all you need to do now is add a division around its center and, using the reference images, work on the overall shape (see Figure 5.92).

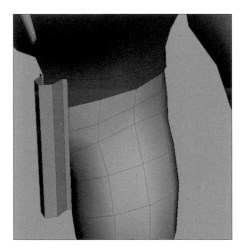

**Figure 5.91**

Duplicate the fold around the Ogre's waist.

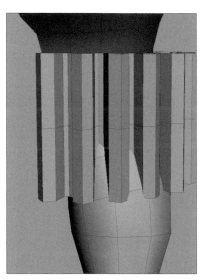

**Figure 5.92**

Add a horizontal division and work on the overall shape.

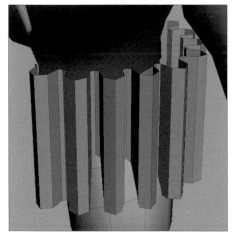

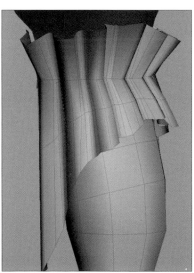

To complete the loin cloth, you can now do some housework and delete each vertical edge loop between each fold (see Figure 5.93). This isn't essential but will help when subdividing the model later.

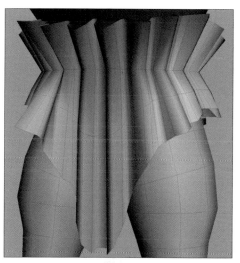

**Figure 5.93**

Finally remove each vertical edge loop from between each fold.

## Accessories

When it comes to accessories like the belt and straps, I like to put these to one side and work on them later. This is mainly because I want to concentrate on the main model. Once that is complete we can accessorize him.

 Now is a good time to save. For reference you can find the file Ogre_08.obj on the companion CD.

## The Final Model

Our base mesh is now complete. We have a good, quaded body, head, shirt, and loin cloth to work upon.

As a game modeler, you are probably wondering about the polygon count. Our Ogre is weighing in at around 6,700 triangles, which is pretty good as it leaves room for his accessories and fur plus any other details we wish to include at a later date.

If you have time, I would recommend leaving this model for a few days and returning to it later with fresh eyes. Then, once you are happy, turn the page and move on to adding UV data.

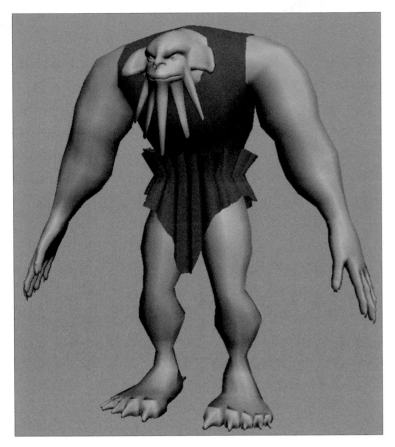 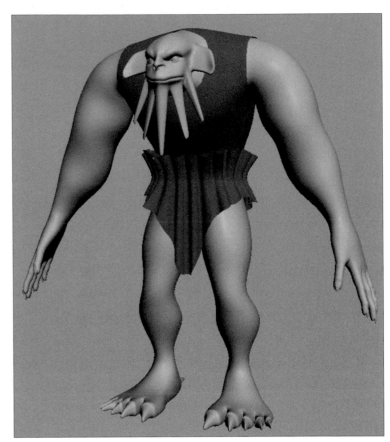

**Figure 5.94** The final base model.

# 6

# UV Mapping

With the base mesh ready, we can now move on to the next stage and apply UV data to it (we will look into what UVs are later in the chapter). Doing this now may cause controversy, since I know that some artists prefer to work a different way, adding UVs to their model after they have sculpted the detail pass. We are trying to save time by retaining our base mesh to use as our final model, whereas some artists prefer to rebuild their base meshes over their detail models—a method sometimes referred to as resurfacing. This is a good way to work because you will ultimately end up with a clean mesh that closely matches the higher-detail model, but it does take time and may result in your doing more work than is actually needed.

With that said, let's proceed and look first at the software I'm using as an example before discussing the different mapping methods.

## Autodesk Maya

As readers of my first book will know, I am a big fan of Maya. I have been using it now for over seven years and am still discovering new tools and techniques. Unlike Silo, Maya is a 3D package that can do pretty much anything you would want. As well as modeling in polygons, nurbs, and subdivision surfaces, you can use it to animate and render, and it also has a full dynamics system, giving the user access to realistic cloth, hair, and fluids. These are just a few of the features Maya holds; with each new release the list grows as the software is streamlined and improved upon.

Below is the short description of Maya taken from their website, www.autodesk.com.

*Award-winning Autodesk® Maya® software is a powerful, integrated 3D modeling, animation, effects, and rendering solution. Because Maya is based on an open architecture, all your work can be scripted or programmed using a well-documented and comprehensive API (application programming interface), or one of two embedded scripting languages. This, combined with an industry-leading suite of 3D tools, means Maya enables you to realize your creative ideas.*

# Mapping Methods

The actual application of UV coordinates onto a model can be heaven or hell, depending on the tools you use. In the past, all you had was a simple set of projection-based tools that would apply the data via a plane, cylinder, or sphere, giving you a base to work with, yet still taking lots of work.

In this section we will look at UVs and different approaches to applying them.

## What Is UV Mapping?

So what are UVs? They are basically points on a model that store a set of coordinates, usually ranging from 0 to 1, which correspond to a point on the texture page. Each UV lies in the same place as a vertex, so the more vertices you have, the more UVs.

Getting a two-dimensional image onto a three-dimensional object isn't easy, as any of you who have tried to wrap an oddly shaped present will know. But we do have technology on our side, allowing us to peel the surface from the object and roll it out flat so we can paint on it.

## Projection Mapping

The most established method for generating UVs is projection mapping. Using a plane, cylinder, or sphere, the user simply projects the coordinates through the object giving a predictable UV map. You can see examples of these in Figure 6.1. You will also see how the grid texture is distorted in certain areas across the surface, with each square being stretched or squashed.

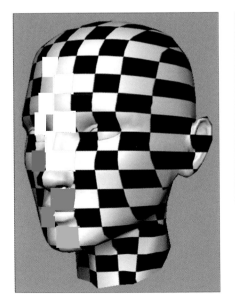 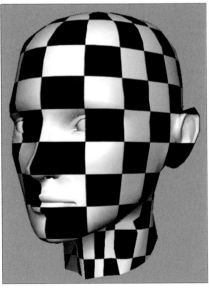 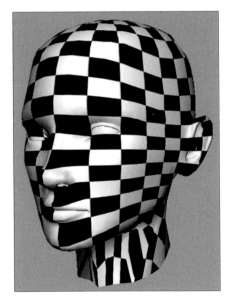

**Figure 6.1**
A head mapped with planar, cylindrical, and spherical projections.

If you open the UV editor, you can see how these projections have affected the UVs. As you can see from Figure 6.2, the first has lots of overlap, with the projection moving directly from the front to the back of the model. The cylindrical and spherical projections have given better, more usable results with minimal overlap in areas such as the ears and nostrils. Of the three, the cylindrical projection is the safer option because the UVs have less distortion, making them easier to paint upon. The only problem is the distortion at the top of the head and around the neck.

As the UVs stand, we would still have more work to do—unfolding and unwrapping the UVs until there is no more overlap and until they are laid out so that there is no (or very minor) texture stretching.

That being said, projection mapping is still one of the best methods for generating a usable UV map and therefore shouldn't be dismissed.

## Pelt Mapping

A more modern technique is pelt mapping and it is now found in most 3D applications. This approach simply relaxes the objects UVs, spreading them out to remove overlap while producing a clean, stretch-free texture. This may sound like the holy grail of UV tools, especially when it can take seconds to produce, but it does have its problems.

Figure 6.3 shows the same head from earlier, but this time the UVs have had the pelt map magic applied.

The grid is clean with little or no distortion, meaning we would have a perfect UV layout, but as you can see in Figure 6.4, it only slightly resembles its parent object.

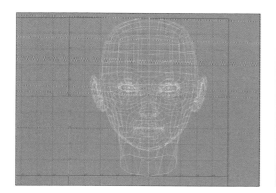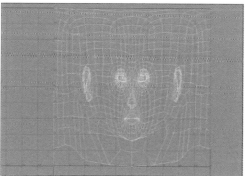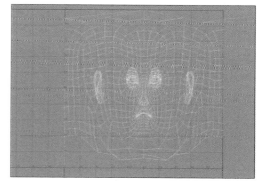

**Figure 6.2** UVs generated using planar, cylindrical, and spherical projections.

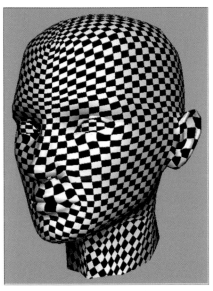

**Figure 6.3**

The head after pelt mapping.

This approach is ideal for objects or characters that rely heavily on a normal map. It will guarantee the best UV layout, meaning better normal map data, but the trade-off would be the difficulty in painting the color map. Areas like the mouth, nose, eyes, and ears could prove troublesome because you would be guessing where the shades and tones would lie.

**Note**

Another option when using pelt mapping is to generate your color maps using a 3D paint program. BodyPaint 3D, Zbrush, and Mudbox all have the ability to paint textures directly onto the 3D model, making for an easy and intuitive way to create your textures.

Projection or pelt: Which approach is best? That comes down to the object being worked on, and the artist's preference. I would, however, suggest using a mixture of both, as we will do in this book with our Ogre.

## UV Preparation

Before we begin let's take a close look at our model and think about how we will texture him. The way we lay out our UVs and the amount of texture space we use are important factors. As with any real-time content, we will have limits to stay within.

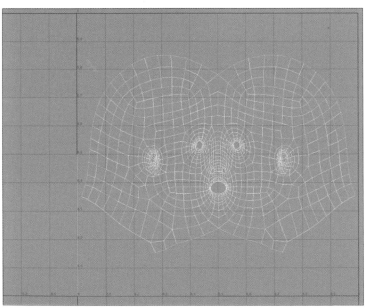

**Figure 6.4** The head UVs after pelt mapping.

## Texture Layout

To save texture space, the obvious thing to do would be to texture half of the Ogre and mirror the model. This would work well, which it has on many models in the past, but can result in the character looking odd and overly symmetrical. One key element to a good character is asymmetry; look at the people around you and you'll notice that what makes them human is that they are not perfectly symmetrical. Differences between their left and right sides make them more interesting and realistic, no matter how subtle those differences are.

You should also consider the game engine itself. We will use normal maps, and some game engines cannot handle mirrored normal maps, so once the character is in game, the normal map will be inverted on the mirrored side, meaning a concave area on one side will be convex on the other, making the character look odd.

Will the game utilize multiple texture passes, meaning a number of materials will be overlaid onto the character? This approach is often used to add dirt or injuries to the character. Any that fell onto his left arm would mirror across to his right. This can be avoided with the use of a second set of UVs, but this can also be expensive, using precious processing power.

We have lots to think about, so let's have a look at our Ogre.

## Dividing the Ogre

Looking at the concept image and the model sheet, I don't think this character would benefit from excessive mirroring. If we keep key areas like his shirt, face, and loin cloth unique, it will open up the ability to add more detail, such as moles, wrinkles, and scars that will improve the overall look of the model. That being said, what we can do initially is generate UVs for half of the

Ogre, and then we can create a duplicate of the areas we want whole, mirroring both the model and its UVs to create a full set.

So we will start by removing half of the model so we are left with the left-hand side, as shown in Figure 6.5.

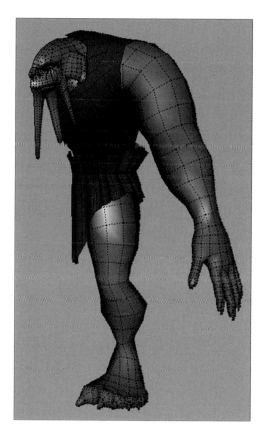

**Figure 6.5**

Remove half of the Ogre.

While we're deleting polygons, we can look at removing some of the now redundant areas under the shirt. These polygons will never be seen, so there is no point in keeping them (see Figure 6.6).

The final step in our preparation is to separate the head, arm, and leg into unique elements; you can see this in Figure 6.7.

Now, before we move on, have a look around the model to make sure there are no triangles or *n*-gons. You can also use this opportunity to tidy up some of the seams if necessary.

The model is now ready for us to begin working on the UVs.

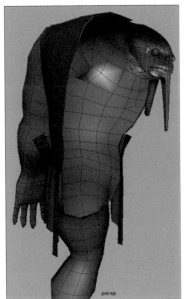
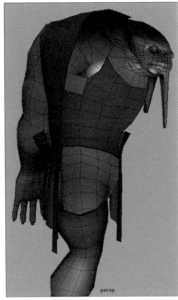

**Figure 6.6**  Remove unused polygons beneath the shirt.

**Figure 6.7**

Separate the head, arm, and leg.

# Applying UVs

It's time to work those UVs and play around with the different mapping techniques to achieve the optimum layout.

## Adding a Checker Texture

To help us while we work with our UVs we need something to apply to our model. Adding a temporary checker map will help visualize how your texture will lie, plus it will highlight areas where the texture would stretch or squash.

Figure 6.8 shows the first checker map. It's a simple black-and-white grid that is fully tile-able. This is almost perfect, but we can do better.

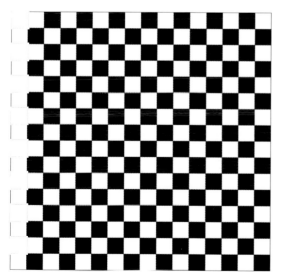

**Figure 6.8**

A basic checker map.

What the black-and-white map won't show are areas where UVs are mirrored or stretching inside each square. For these reasons we turn to the more advanced map pictured in Figure 6.9.

**Figure 6.9**

A more advanced checker map.

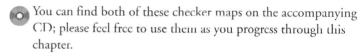 You can find both of these checker maps on the accompanying CD; please feel free to use them as you progress through this chapter.

## Head

I always start with the head on a character because it is usually the most important and trickiest area to work with. This character is no exception with his odd-shaped head, large ears, and beard.

Let's look at the head on its own (see Figure 6.10). It looks like we may have to divide this further to make our job of mapping it easier. The obvious things to do would be to detach his ear and beard, but we must be careful of seams.

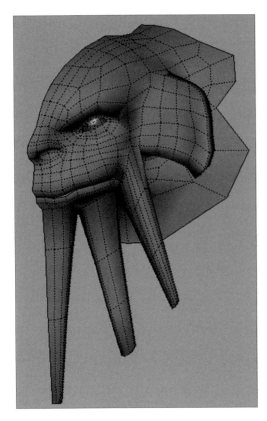

**Figure 6.10**

This head is a rather complicated shape, so we must divide it further before we can map it.

Texture seams are unavoidable, but we can try to make them less obvious by hiding them, or by placing them across areas where the texture isn't complicated. What you must also take into consideration are levels of detail. These are lower-resolution versions of the model that are used when the character is further from the game camera and are usually generated by optimizing the main model. If you place a seam incorrectly, when you reduce the polygons in that area, you may drastically affect the seam such that the texture doesn't join correctly, making the seam more obvious.

Because this head is such a tricky shape, we will enlist the help of a pelt map. This will give good UV coverage, but we will need to make a few preparations first.

1. To begin, apply the checker map to our model. Because the head currently has no UVs, the material may not show up.

2. Next detach the beard and ear and hide them (Figure 6.11).

## Pelt Mapping Seams

When generating a pelt map, you are usually required to specify seams in the model. Seams are areas that can be unstitched, allowing the UVs to relax easier and generate a smoother UV map. In the case of our Ogre, these will be added at the top of his head and under his chin, allowing the sides of his head to unfold without pinching or overlap.

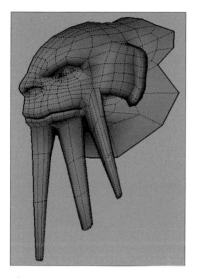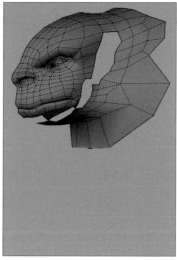

**Figure 6.11** To pelt map the head, first detach and hide the beard and ear.

3. If we generated the pelt map now, it would resemble that in Figure 6.12. We can just make out the eye and nostril, but the rest is a bit of a mess. This comes down to two things: the fact that this is just half a head, and the holes left when we removed the ear and beard. When a pelt map is generated, it tries to retain the shape of each polygon, not allowing it to stretch or be squashed. Because we have holes in our model, there is nothing to retain the shape, so the pelt map opens up the UVs.

4. Let's fix some of the problems now, before we reapply our pelt map. First fill in the holes under his chin, and on the side of his head, (see Figure 6.13). These will just be temporary fixes; as will remove the geometry again once the map is complete.

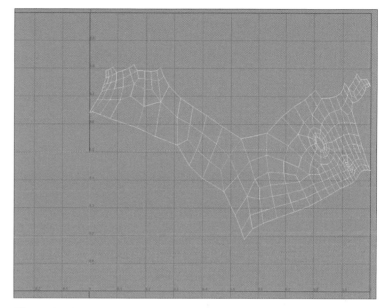

**Figure 6.12** A pelt map applied to the current head.

5. Next we will mirror the head, making it whole again. The pelt map should be much cleaner, easier to read and more symmetrical.

6. Now if you reapply the pelt map, you should have something close to that shown in Figure 6.14. It's looking much better, but the wide-open mouth area is not working at all.

7. Quickly filling in the mouth before reapplying our pelt map gives a much more agreeable result, as you can see in Figure 6.15.

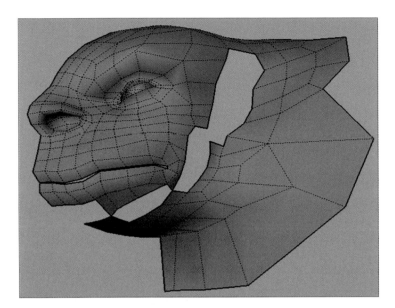

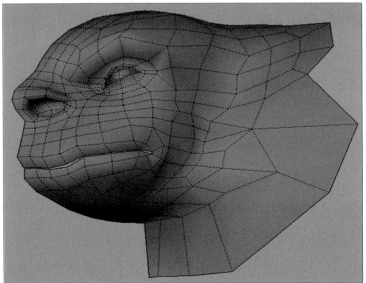

**Figure 6.13** First fill in the holes around the head.

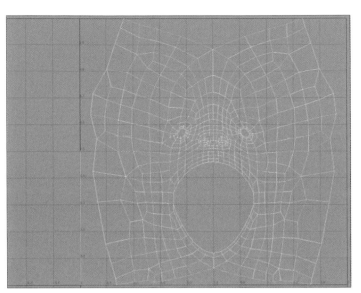

**Figure 6.14** The pelt reapplied to the head, but we still need to fix the mouth.

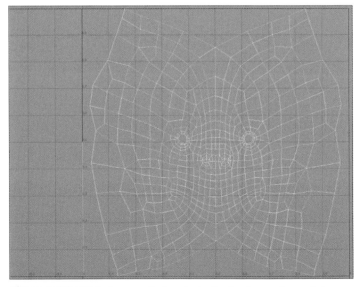

**Figure 6.15** With the mouth closed, the final pelt map is much improved.

Looking to our model now, you can see how the texture is laid out. Apart from the UVs needing to be mirrored, we have a decent layout with a few problem areas where the grid is distorted, as you can see in Figure 6.16.

**Figure 6.16**

The current UV layout still has some minor issues.

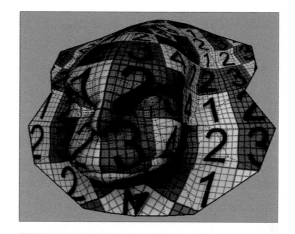

As it stands, you could happily use this set of UVs, but I would recommend taking some time to work on them further to try and achieve a smoother layout.

Figure 6.17 shows the final head map. Yes, it still has some distortion, but on a shape like this, removing all of it would be nearly impossible.

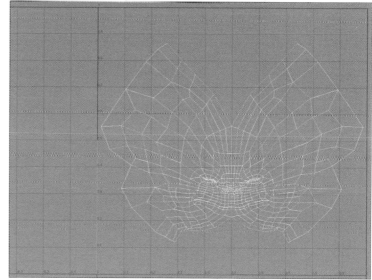

**Figure 6.17** Working further on the UVs will help reduce the distortion.

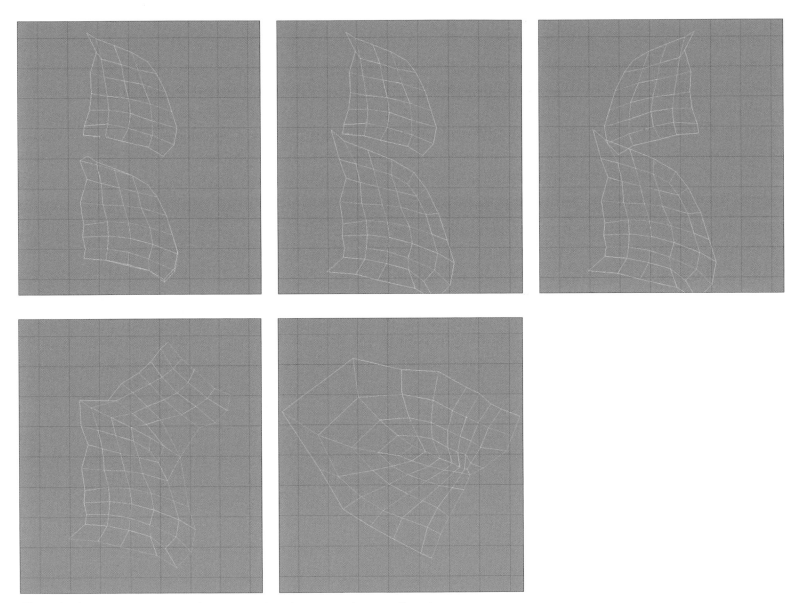

**Figure 6.18** Work with the UVs of the ear to reduce the seams and texture distortion.

Now we can look at the remaining parts of the head, but before we do, make sure you delete the polygons that you added in earlier to help with the pelt map.

The ear should be a simpler shape to map, and you can probably get away with having just one seam hidden beneath it.

1. Focus in on the ear and apply a basic planar projection to the front.

2. Detach the polygons on the rear of the ear so they are a separate element, and switch to the UV editor.

3. Move the UVs for the back of the ear above the ones for the front, like in Figure 6.18.

4. The texture on the sides of the model will be stretched due to the projection. Move the UVs out to fix this. You could even select them all and scale them outward (see Figure 6.18).

5. Finally, the UVs on the rear of the ear will be reversed, so quickly flip these so the texture is correct.

6. To attempt to hide the seam, now stitch the UVs across the top of the ear.

7. As with the head, now that you have a good basic layout, it would be a good idea to rework some of the UVs to smooth out the texture and maybe even stitch a bit more of the seam.

We are almost done with the head; as you can see in Figure 6.19, all that remains is his beard.

**Figure 6.19** The head and ear are mapped.

For these elements simple cylindrical maps will do, with a bit of tweaking afterward. Just make sure the seams lie behind each piece.

Once done, mirror the beard sections and the ear to fill out the right side of the head, making sure you also mirror the UVs so the numbers in the texture are the right way.

For the central beard you will need to weld the geometry as well as the UVs. See Figure 6.20.

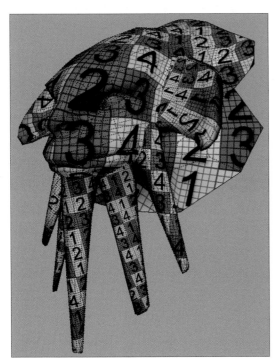

**Figure 6.20**

The mapped head.

## Hand and Arm

Things should get a little easier from now on, so let's move onto the hand. At present, the hand and arm are all one object, so to make mapping easier, we need to divide it into manageable elements.

1. To begin with, first detach the hand and hide the arm (see Figure 6.21).

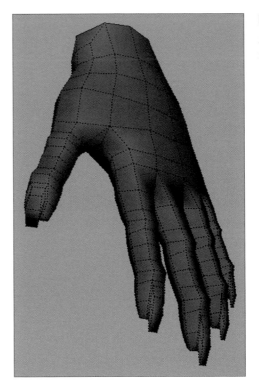

**Figure 6.21**

Separate the hand from the arm.

2. The hand is basically flat, meaning a simple planar projection map will work, but we need the top and bottom to be mapped separately. First select the faces making up the underneath of the hand and detach them to a separate element. As shown in Figure 6.22, create the break across the center of each finger and thumb, following the edges so the top and bottom of each digit are equal.

3. Apply a planar projection through the hand. As you can see from Figure 6.23, this gives a good layout with only a few minor tweaks needed between each finger to reduce the stretching. Turning the model slightly, we can also see that we need to work on the thumb.

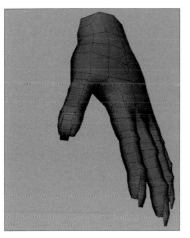 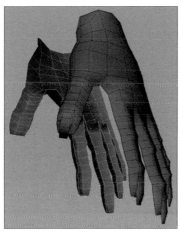

**Figure 6.22** Detach the bottom of the hand.

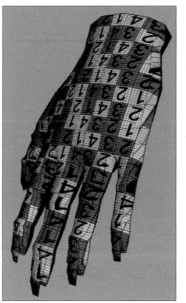 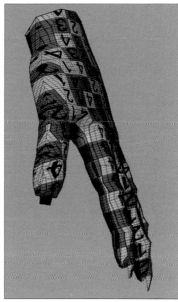

**Figure 6.23** Apply a planar projection to both pieces of the hand.

4. As you can see in Figure 6.24, all that is needed to fix the fingers and thumb is some small adjustments to the UVs. Moving the points out at either side of each finger and unfolding the thumb will reduce the stretching.

> **Note**
>
> It's important to make sure the UVs do not overlap.

Figure 6.25 shows the edited UVs. As you can see, we have now removed the stretched areas.

 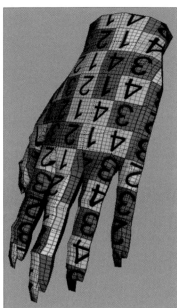

**Figure 6.25** The hand minus the stretching around the fingers and thumb.

5. Now apply the same procedure underneath the hand, moving the UVs out to reduce the stretching on the texture (see Figure 6.26). You will also need to mirror the UVs because the texture will initially be reversed.

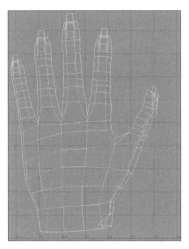 

**Figure 6.24** Move the outer UVs out from each digit to reduce the texture stretching.

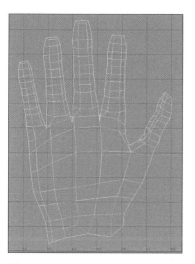
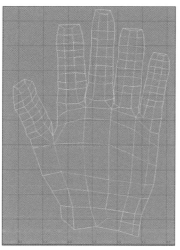

**Figure 6.26** Next rework the UVs underneath the hand.

We will leave the hand at this stage and move on to the arm. Simply apply a cylindrical map to this piece of geometry, making sure the seam lies underneath, running from the armpit to the wrist. Once the projection is applied, you will need to tweak the overall UV layout to smooth out the texture.

You can see the arm and its UVs in Figure 6.27.

**Note**

A pelt map will also work on the arm; just make sure the seam lies hidden beneath.

If you look at Figure 6.28, the completed arm and hand, you can see that we have an obvious seam around the wrist. What we will do now is stitch the hand UVs to the arm, removing the seam.

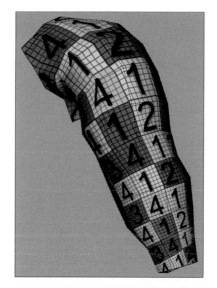

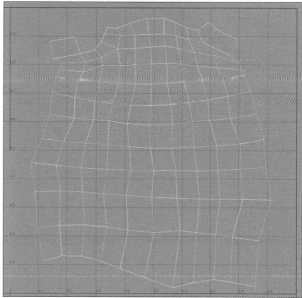

**Figure 6.27** Apply a simple cylindrical map to the arm, making sure the seam lies underneath.

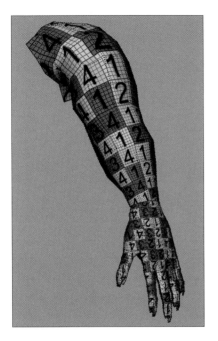

**Figure 6.28**

Our hand and arm are mapped, but there is a seam around the wrist.

1. To stitch these elements, we first need to recombine the upper hand, lower hand, and the arm.

2. With the pieces combined, switch to your UV editor. As you can see in Figure 6.29, the layout is a bit of a mess at present.

3. First separate the hand and arm UVs.

4. Next stitch the upper hand to the arm, making sure the UVs are smooth with no stretching.

5. Now attach the lower hand to the arm, again editing the joining UVs.

6. Finally we can stitch the upper and lower little finger UVs, removing the seam across the side of the hand.

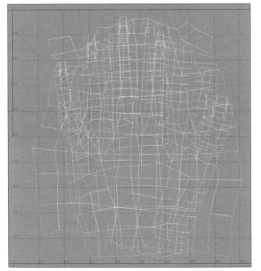
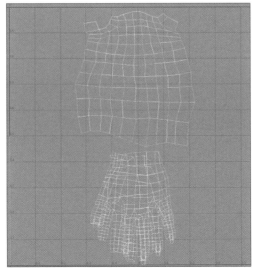
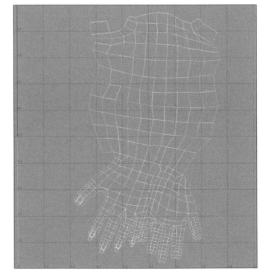

**Figure 6.29** Stitch the hand and arm UVs to reduce the amount of seams.

We have now removed the seam from the wrist and smoothed out the flow of the texture down the arm and onto the hand (see Figure 6.30).

Now before we finish with the arm, we can do one last thing. To help add definition to the hands, let's add new UVs to each finger nail. This will bring them out of each finger, allowing us to add more detail to them, which will make the hand look more realistic.

1. Following Figure 6.31, first detach each finger nail, separating it from each finger.

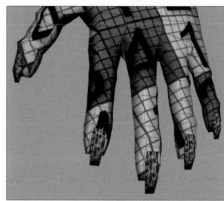

**Figure 6.31**

Detach each finger nail and apply a planar projection.

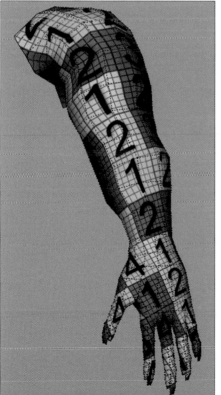

**Figure 6.30**

The full arm with UVs.

2. Apply a basic planar projection to each nail.

3. As shown in Figure 6.32, move to your UV editor and unfold each nail so you don't have any overlapping UVs.

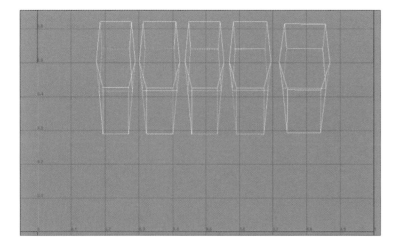

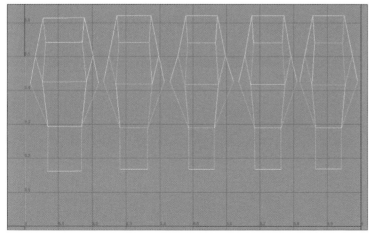

**Figure 6.32** Unfold the UVs to remove overlap.

That's all; the arm, hand, and finger nails are complete.

You may be wondering why we didn't simply opt for a pelt map for these elements. Well, first, adding UVs this way was a good example of using projection-based mapping. But I suppose the main reason behind the course we took in this section is that we need to have the finger UVs clear and easily readable for when we paint in the detail later, and applying a pelt map would have bunched the finger UVs, making it difficult to add detail into each digit.

## Foot and Leg

Let's move on to the foot and leg next. You could try to map these in a similar way to the hand, but for this area we can comfortably use a pelt map because we won't lose any detail in the toes since they are short and stumpy.

1. As with the hand, we will map the claws separately, so begin by detaching and hiding them (see Figure 6.33).

2. As illustrated in Figure 6.34, using your pelt-mapping tool of choice, add a seam down the inner leg and then around the foot and across the toes, but leave the outer foot free.

3. Now when you press your "Pelt" button, you should end up with something similar to that in Figure 6.35.

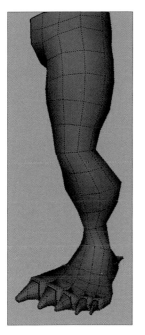
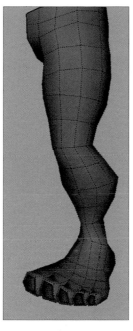

**Figure 6.33**

First detach and hide the claws.

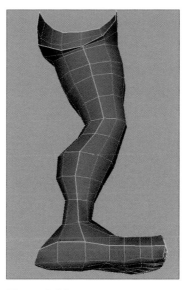
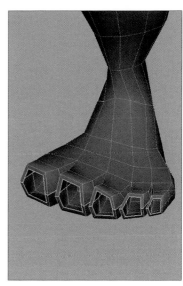

**Figure 6.34** Add the pelt-mapping seams down the inner leg and across the foot.

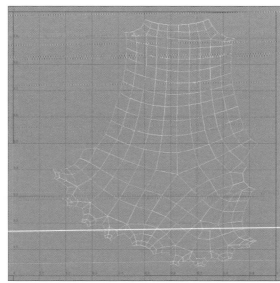

**Figure 6.35**

The leg successfully pelt mapped.

That's the leg done, so now let's map the claws. We can approach these any number of ways. You could use pelt mapping again with the seam underneath each claw, or you could map them cylindrically. At this stage I will leave the choice in your hands, but you can see the mapped claws and their UVs in Figure 6.36 and Figure 6.37.

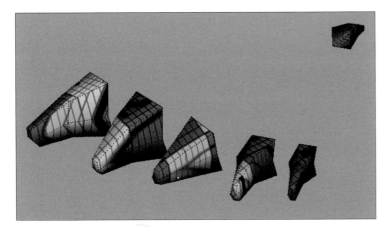

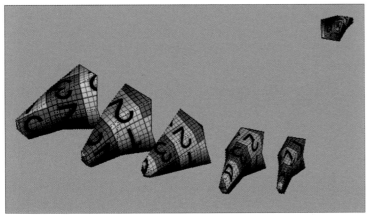

**Figure 6.36**  The mapped claws.

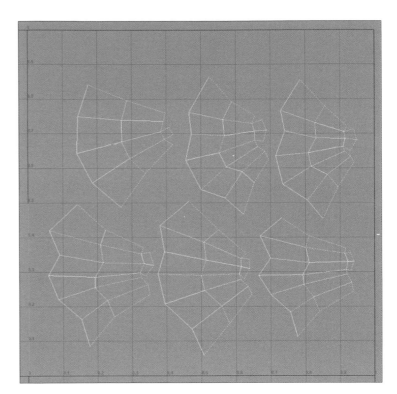

**Figure 6.37**  The claw UVs.

## Clothing

The final sections to map are the Ogre's shirt and loin cloth. Since these are simple shapes, the best approach would be to pelt map them as we did with the leg.

Let's look at the shirt first. At present we have only half the shirt, but we will need the full garment so we can add more detail, and so the pelt map will unfold correctly.

1. To start, simply mirror the shirt and combine the new half with the original (see Figure 6.38).

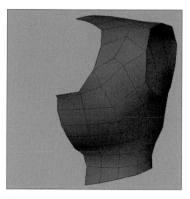
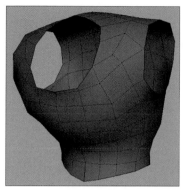

**Figure 6.38** Duplicate and mirror the original half of the shirt.

2. Next fire up your pelt-mapping tool of choice and create two seams down either side of the shirt. You can see these in Figure 6.39. We create the seams here firstly because shirts tend to have seams here, but also because when the arm is in its rest position, the seams will be hidden.

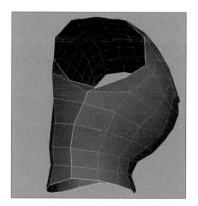
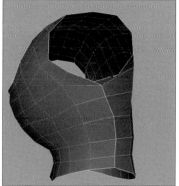

**Figure 6.39** Create two seams down either side of the shirt.

3. When the pelt map is complete, your shirt should resemble that in Figure 6.40, with its UVs nicely spaced and spread out.

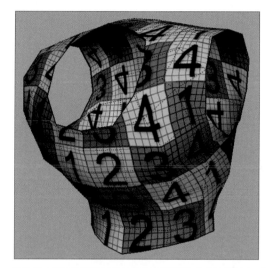

**Figure 6.40**

The final pelt-mapped shirt and UVs.

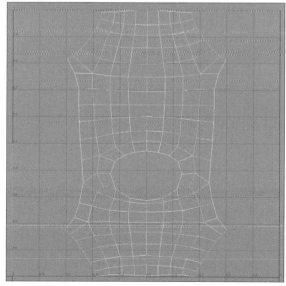

With the loin cloth we will rely on mapping one half of it. We can do this because we don't need much detail added into the textures as we have the folds in the geometry. However, to make sculpting easier, we will need the full object, so we can repeat the steps above to quickly pelt map it.

1. Begin by duplicating the existing side of the loin cloth, mirroring it, and combining it with the original (see Figure 6.41).

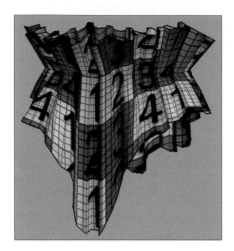

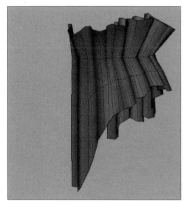

**Figure 6.41**  Duplicate the loin cloth to make the right side.

2. Because we are using only one half of the loin cloth, we can't place the seams down each side. Instead, place a single seam down the back, marking the center of the object.

3. Once pelted, your object should look like that in Figure 6.42.

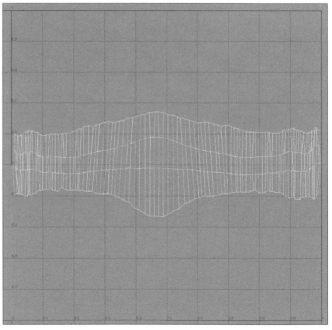

**Figure 6.42**  The final pelt-mapped loin cloth and UVs.

That's the first step complete, and you can see our mapped Ogre in Figure 6.43. Now that we have the UVs applied, we have to arrange them into texture pages.

**Figure 6.43**

The mapped Ogre.

# UV Layout

It's time to put the pieces of the puzzle together and compile our texture pages. But before you begin, you must have a good idea of the texture pages you are allowed to use. Whether it be a single 1k (1024 x 1024) page, two larger pages, or multiple smaller pages, you will have limits to stay within. These limits are dictated mainly by the hardware in the target console, but the actual game itself will have an influence. For example, if our Ogre is to remain in the third-person perspective (camera behind and slightly above the character) with the player never being close to him, we can have smaller textures, but if the player will be close to the creature, we will need to see more detail, so the pages will need to be larger.

With all this in mind, let's look at our character. As he is being created for the purposes of this book and will probably never make it into a game, we can be more relaxed with the textures, but we don't want to create more work for ourselves. We will use two 2k textures (each 2048 x 2048). One will hold all the skin-toned areas—head, arm, leg, etc.—while the other can be used for his clothing and accessories. Using this configuration will also be good for future versions of the model, if, for example, we need a new skin color or different clothing.

Let's look at our model. Looking at Figure 6.44, our current UV layout is very messy. Applying a quick and dirty layout procedure cleans up the scene, but the claws are now taking up most of the page, which is wrong.

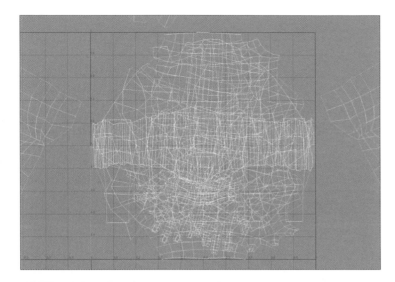

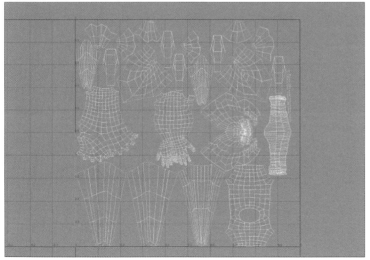

**Figure 6.44** Arrange the messy UVs so they don't overlap.

**Note**

If your 3D application doesn't have the ability to quickly lay out the UV's shells, then you will have to move and scale them by hand.

Our first job now is to arrange the UV shells in order of priority. Areas like his head, torso, and limbs need to take up more space on the page compared to his claws; they need more details and are viewed more often. To help us do this, we can use the checker map as a guide.

Figure 6.45 shows our current UV layout and how the texture is represented on the model. The texture is of varying sizes depending on the element it is covering, but what we want ideally is for the grid to be spaced similarly over the Ogre's body.

Keeping in mind which elements need to be on what texture pages, start to adjust each UV shell, simply moving, rotating, or scaling each piece while trying to keep the texture a similar size overall.

Aim for a layout like that in Figure 6.46.

**Note**

It's important to leave a little space between the UV's shells. If the texture page is eventually made smaller, you may end up with areas bleeding into each other across the seams.

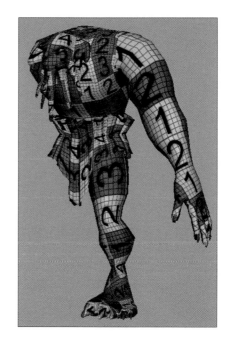

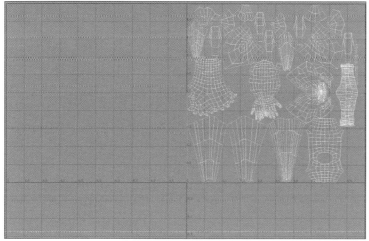

**Figure 6.45** The Ogre before the UV layout.

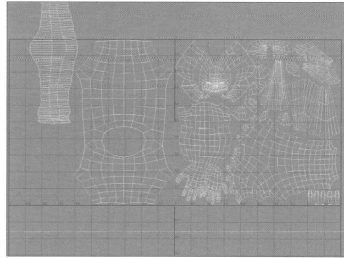

**Figure 6.46** The final UV layout.

One thing you may be wondering is why the loin cloth UVs are falling out of the grid. Well, we are only planning on using half the model of the loin cloth, mirroring it for the other side. Keeping the object whole for now will help when we come to sculpt, but we don't need the left side's UVs, so we can leave them out of the texture page.

Next we will stop being technical and actually become artists as we start to sculpt in the details.

For reference you can find the final file Ogre_09.obj on the companion CD.

# 7

# Virtual Sculpting

With our base mesh complete and UV data applied, we can now move on to the fun part and add some much-needed detail to this plain-looking model. In this chapter we will explore the world of virtual sculpting as we apply what is commonly known as the "detail pass."

It's important to add that this chapter will not cover each brush stroke. As you can appreciate, this would not only make for a painfully long chapter but also a mind-numbing read. Instead we will look at each part in turn and illustrate the main steps taken to achieve the final result.

## Introduction to Sculpting

Virtual sculpting is exactly what the name suggests. You take a low-resolution model, which acts like a lump of clay, subdivide it a few times to increase the density of the mesh, and, using a brush, you pull, push, pinch, scratch, etc., at the surface to build up detail. The denser the model, the more details you can apply. It's a very easy and intuitive way of working, allowing the game artist to get maximum results in a fraction of the time manual modeling would take.

A few packages exist that focus on this process (ZBrush and Mudbox are the main two), with many others adding the ability to sculpt geometry into their toolsets. Boiled down, they are all very similar and work more or less the same way, with each adding new and improved workflow to each release.

### Tip

To get the best from your sculpting application, I would recommend splurging on a decent graphics tablet like the ones created by Wacom. A mouse can be very restrictive, whereas a pen will allow you to create smooth strokes in a more natural way. These tablets can range in price and size, so don't be scared into thinking you need an expensive A3 one. Saying that, the good ones that allow for maximum control and sensitivity, like the Wacom Intuos 3, can be pricey but well worth the money. As for size, I would stick to A4 unless you absolutely need to go bigger.

# Brushes

Brushes form the foundation of the sculpting toolset. The basic brushes usually include a *Soft* brush, shown in Figure 7.1, which paints smooth strokes; a *Smooth* brush, which averages out the vertices, in effect smoothing the surface; a *Pinch* brush, which pulls the surface together to help create creases; and also a *Move* brush, which allows you to rework the base model to adjust proportions and form.

With these simple brushes you could easily work your way around your model, adjusting the brush size to make broader or narrower strokes, adjusting the fall off to soften or harden the brush, and switching between the default pull to a push at the press of a button to add recessed areas. Thankfully though, we are now presented with many other brushes, and with ZBrush's last release came some impressive brushes to help add stitches, rivets, and even a basic eye shape with the click of a stylus.

# Stencils

Another important tool in the sculpting environment is stencils. Taking a mask made from a basic grayscale image, the user can project his brush strokes through the image, transferring its detail onto the surface. As you can see from Figure 7.2, this can be a quick way to add details in a matter of minutes that would have otherwise taken hours of work.

There are many other tools we could talk about, including masking, symmetry, and layers, but they would take a book in themselves to explain and it would involve going deeper into specific packages. Instead, let's move on and look at the application I have chosen to use in this section.

  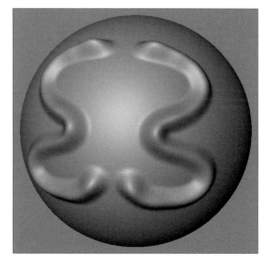

**Figure 7.1** The effect of the Soft brush and symmetrical sculpting.

**Figure 7.2**

A basic sphere with surface detail added with the help of stencils.

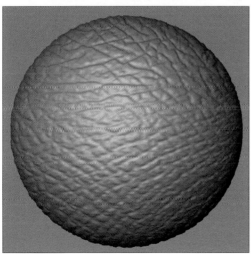

# Autodesk Mudbox

A relatively new application in the 3D world is Mudbox. Here is the marketing description from the Autodesk website:

> *Autodesk® Mudbox™ is the first advanced, high resolution brush-based 3D sculpting software that is built from the ground up to address the needs of the professional digital sculptor.*

> *Designed by production artists for production artists, Mudbox introduces new ideas and combines familiar concepts in fresh ways to offer a unique solution for high-end commercial modeling and design.*

> *With its friendly interface, consistent structure, respect for industry convention, and a "get it done" focus, Mudbox is quick to learn and easy to use, integrating seamlessly with existing pipelines. Digital artists with previous 3D experience are quickly productive in Mudbox with minimal or even no orientation.*

You may be wondering why I have opted to use Mudbox when ZBrush has been around longer and is the more established package. Quite simply, Mudbox is great to use, and more importantly for the purposes of this book and the people reading it, it's a pick-up-and-sculpt package.

On first loading ZBrush, the user can feel intimidated by its complicated interface. Add to this the awkward workflow, how objects are treated like tools, and so on, and it could be a few days before you find yourself settling in. Don't get me wrong; I think ZBrush is an excellent package and, given time, you can create some amazing pieces with it. Using Mudbox, however, with its much cleaner and simpler interface, you can be up and running in a few minutes. You load in your object, subdivide it, and start sculpting...easy as that.

# Let's Sculpt

So enough chatter; let's move on and start sculpting. But first you need to divide the Ogre and export each section as a wavefront .obj file. This is the standard format for models and is used by most, if not all, 3D and sculpting applications.

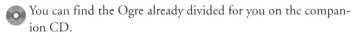 You can find the Ogre already divided for you on the companion CD.

**Note**

You could bring the entire model into your application and work on it whole, but as you subdivide it and the polygon count rises, you will find it increasingly difficult to work as each movement will become slow and labored.

**Tip**

Before you begin sculpting, have a good idea in your head of your target texture page resolution. If your page is to be quite small, you can ignore the later details like small wrinkles and even skin detail as they will be lost in translation. This sort of detail should be left for main characters where the model will be seen close up onscreen.

# Arm and Hand

I find it best to start with the more difficult areas first, so that as you work, things get a little easier. Let's begin with the arm and the hand.

**Note**

It's important before you proceed that you have ample muscle reference at hand. This could be from a book or just images you have grabbed from the Internet, but you will need to see how muscles flow as you work.

1. Following Figure 7.3, first bring your model into the sculpting package.

2. It's looking a little boxy and plain, so let's add a division to smooth it out before starting to work in the main muscle shapes. At this stage, simply use a soft brush, gently smoothing each stroke when the basic shape is in place.

3. When you are happy, add a further division and continue to work in more detail. Take the opportunity to rework the proportions using the Move brush, thickening up the wrist, hand, and fingers.

**Note**

As you can probably tell from the figures, the arm's shape changes quite a bit as it is sculpted. When sculpting, don't be afraid to change the shape if something looks incorrect; in this case, the deltoid had much more definition than was needed.

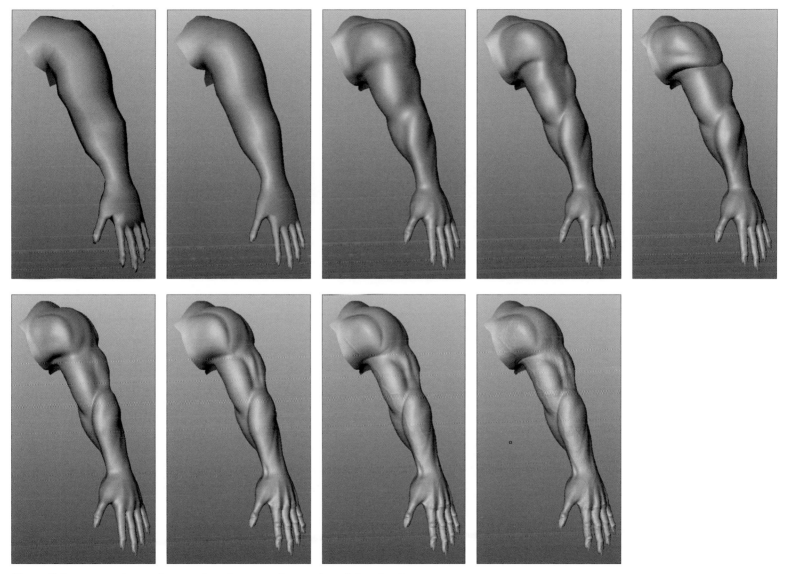

**Figure 7.3** Bring in the arm base mesh and paint in the muscle and skin detail.

4. Continue to work in more detail, now moving down to the hand. Give the Ogre large knuckles and add definition to the finger nails.

5. Jump up another division level and paint in veins as well as the tendons beneath the wrist. Again, all we are doing at this stage is painting and smoothing.

6. Add a final division and, using an appropriate stencil, add some much-needed detail to the skin to break up the smooth surface.

### Note

Try to keep your division levels to around six; any more than this at this stage would be a waste and make working with the arm difficult. Six divisions are ample for the amount of detail we need at this stage.

That's the arm pretty much done. As you can imagine, building this amount of detail manually would have taken days, and sculpting it should have taken only a few hours.

Before we continue, look at our stages in Figure 7.4. Here you can see the gradual progression taken as the arm is divided. Now let's turn our attention to Figure 7.5.

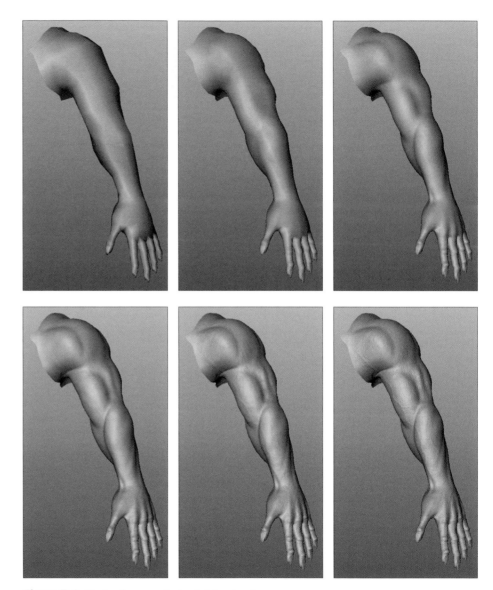

**Figure 7.4** Each of our arm's six division levels.

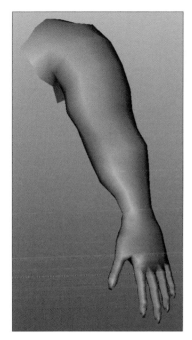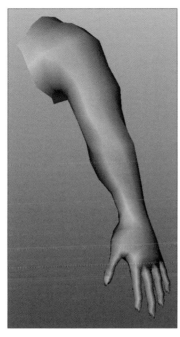

**Figure 7.5** After sculpting, the base mesh's shape has changed to fit the new detail.

Figure 7.5 shows the base mesh both before and after we applied the detail pass. As you can see, the shape has changed as we have worked. This is because each modification is passed down through the hierarchy, altering the lower stages. This is a good thing because you can use the new base mesh in our final model, as it closely matches the detail pass, making it perfect when you come to extract and apply the normal map later.

# Leg and Foot

We will approach the leg and foot in pretty much the same way as the arm. As you proceed you will notice a pattern emerging, one of working on each level of division fully before moving on to the next. This is possibly the best way to approach sculpting, since working from the highest level down could prove troublesome when you try to add larger muscles.

> **Note**
>
> Notice that the leg model in this section is slightly different from the one in the previous chapter. To help achieve the best results you should include the right-hand side of the pelvis, even if it is to be discarded later. This is to help keep the overall shape when the model is subdivided.

1. Start a new scene and bring in the leg base model.

2. Following Figure 7.6, add a division and begin to work in the main muscles, including the knee cap.

3. When you move to the pelvis area, it would be a good idea to enable symmetrical painting, if the option is available. This will copy any strokes made on one side of the model to the other. In this case, we will eventually discard the right side of his pelvis, so it will be important that when mirrored later, the pelvis matches seamlessly.

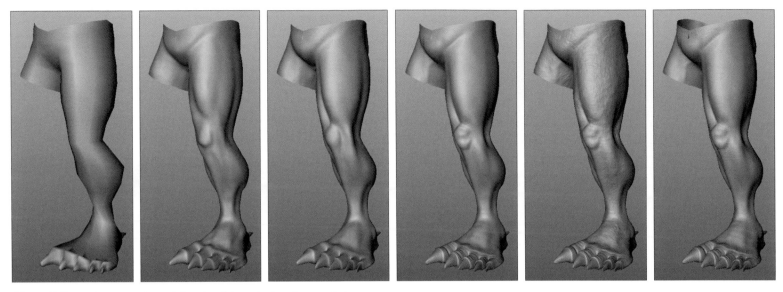

**Figure 7.6** Work in muscle and skin detail into the leg, foot, and claws.

4. Continue to refine the model, adding creases into the toes and even working grain into the claws.

5. Once you reach division six, use a stencil similar to that for the arm to add skin detail. This will help to break up the surface.

### Creases and Folds

When you work with clothed models, it's important to step back and consider your approach. When characters are in game, their arms are lowered, with their knees and elbows being bent most of the time. To prepare for this, sculpt creases and folds into the cloth to reflect this so they will look correct when running around onscreen.

The leg is complete; feel free to work on it further should you wish to add more wrinkles or other details.

Figure 7.7 shows the resulting stages that form the leg.

## Head

To sculpt detail into the head, we can enlist the help of the symmetry tool again. Although we won't be removing half of the head, this tool will help save time initially and give us a good base to work upon.

1. As illustrated in Figure 7.8, bring the head base mesh into a new scene.

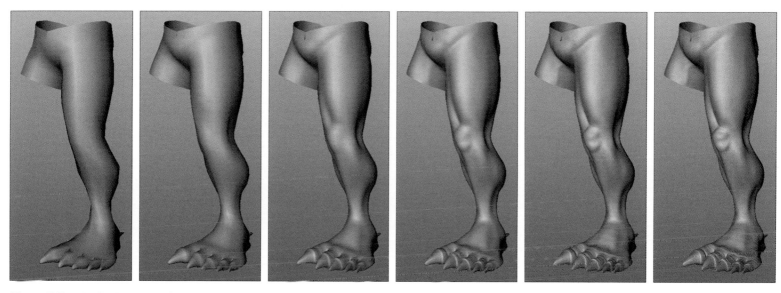

**Figure 7.7** The final stages of the leg detail pass.

2. Making sure symmetry is enabled, begin to work the details into the left side of his head. At this early stage, also consider the shape of his eyes, nose, and mouth, making any changes that are needed to fit the concept image.

3. Stepping up a level, next add detail into the beard as well as working on the wrinkles around the eyes.

4. When you're happy, add a new division. This will allow you to work on the eyebrows as well as add basic hair strokes to the top of his head.

**Tip**

To help visualize the overall head, add some basic eye geometry. This will also aid when working with the shape of the outer eye.

5. Time to turn off the symmetry tool and include some variety to either side of the head. Begin to add moles, wrinkles, and creases to his face, and vary the hair strokes.

6. With the final division, work in the skin detail using stencils to help, as in Figure 7.9.

7. To finish, raise the top of the head to add volume to the hair and then vary the beard to relax the shape.

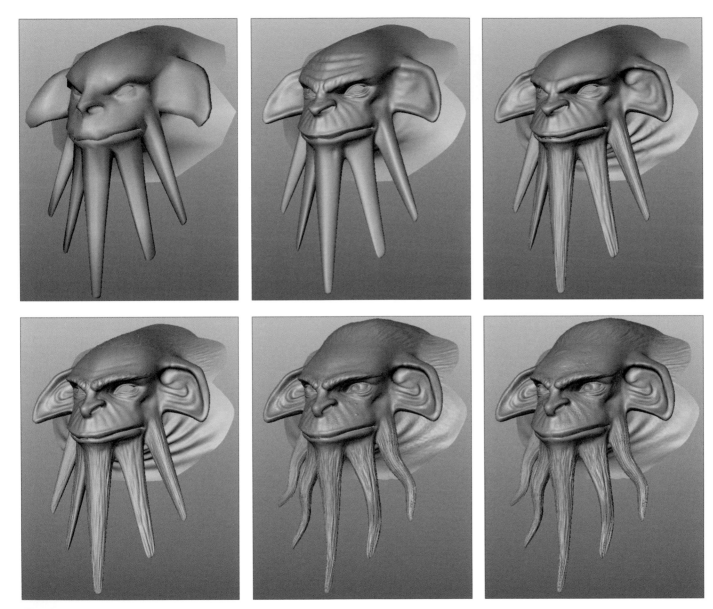

**Figure 7.8** Use the symmetry brush initially to add detail into the head.

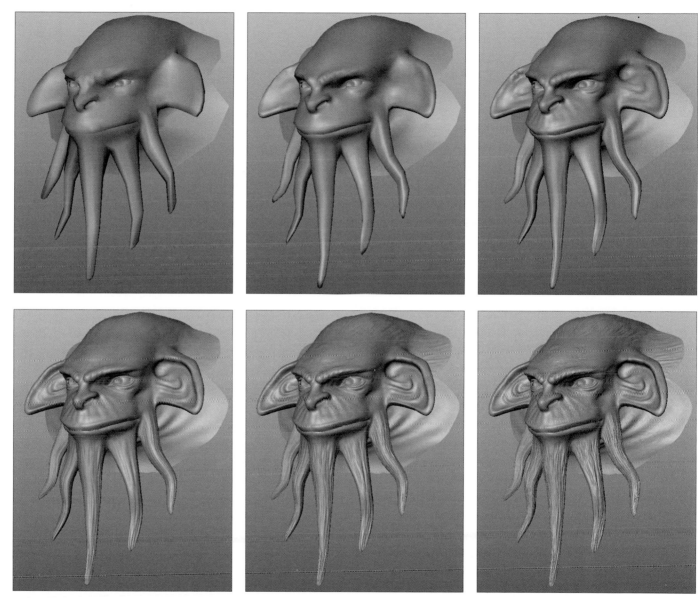

**Figure 7.9** The final stages of the head detail pass.

# Clothing

As promised, the clothing should be easier to sculpt, especially since by now you should be coming to grips with sculpting.

Let's begin with the shirt. You might be thinking that we will use the symmetry tool here too, but you would be wrong. To start off, we need to create the base creases that will fall across the shirt, making it asymmetrical.

1. As demonstrated in Figure 7.10, import the shirt base mesh and add two subdivisions.

2. Next paint in some broad creases across the front of the shirt, remembering to create some that fall under each arm and around the base.

3. With the basics in place, we can now add some variety with the help of a stencil.

4. The Ogre's shirt is made from fur, and at this stage it would be good to use a layer if your package has them. Layers allow you to sculpt detail while restricting it to the selected layer. Much like in Adobe Photoshop, this layer can then be turned invisible and even have its opacity altered without affecting the rest of the model. With symmetry enabled, apply short brushstrokes all over the shirt to give it a look of fur.

5. Now turn off symmetry and paint some variety to each side.

6. The fur currently looks a little too harsh, so play around with the layer's opacity, and even smooth the strokes to soften the effect.

Finally we have the loin cloth. The plan for this model was to split and mirror it later, so it would be sensible to use the symmetry brush while keeping in mind that the right side of it will be discarded.

1. Bring in the base mesh and subdivide to smooth out the shape.

2. Begin to work in some detail, adding variety and texture to the model while also emphasizing the upper and lower seams.

3. Finish off by using a stencil to add smaller surface detail (Figure 7.11).

The main sections are now complete. We will need to create the accessories later, but for those we won't be using a sculpting package to add detail, instead we will explore the use of plug-ins to generate normal maps in the following chapter.

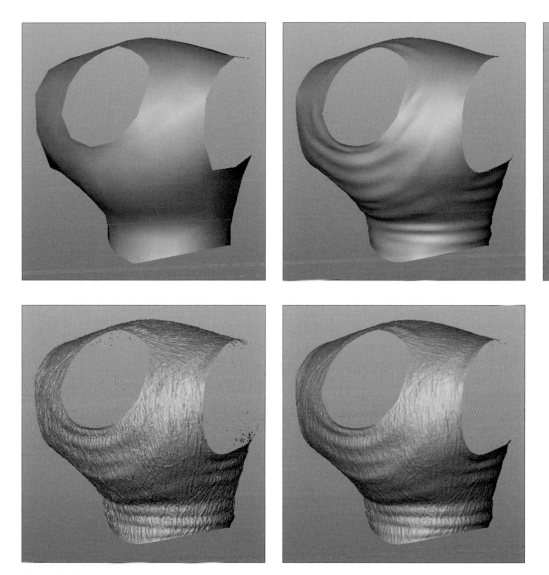

**Figure 7.10**  Paint in detail to the shirt, using a layer to help with the fur effect.

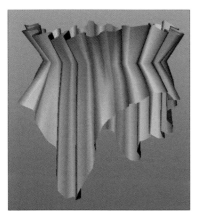 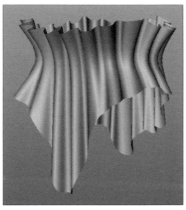 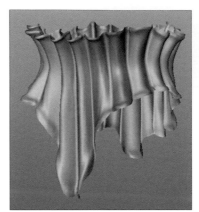 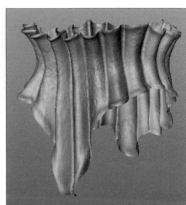

**Figure 7.11** Finally, add detail to the loin cloth.

## All Together Now

Take a breather and admire your work. Your final mode should look something like that in Figure 7.12.

There are areas we could tweak, or even work on further. The shirt, for example, still looks a little harsh, but we can tweak the normal maps later to soften this when we can see them on the actual game model. Alternatively, if the texture page will be resized, this will also help to soften some of the harsher details.

## Resurface

With the detail pass complete, many people now choose to rebuild the base mesh using the higher-resolution version as a guide. This can work well to help produce a clean model that closely matches the high-resolution mesh but can take time you don't have and may feel like you are repeating work you did earlier. As well as rebuilding the base mesh, you will also need to

reapply the UVs, but to be honest, if your intention was to resurface, you could have skipped the earlier UV pass.

Resurfacing can be achieved by exporting the high-resolution model and taking it into a 3D package that includes surface snapping, such as Silo or Softimage XSI. This allows the user to build up a lower-resolution model by snapping each new vertex to the surface of the high-resolution model.

Another great tool for this in Silo is the Topology brush, mentioned briefly in Chapter 2. With this brush, you simply draw on your high-resolution model and Silo generates a model from the lines.

For this model we will not be resurfacing; instead we will use the lowest-level geometry from our sculptures, taking these into a 3D package to use as a base for our in-game model. Before that, however, let's turn our attention to detail textures.

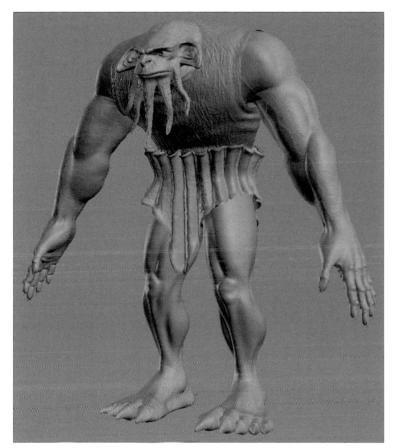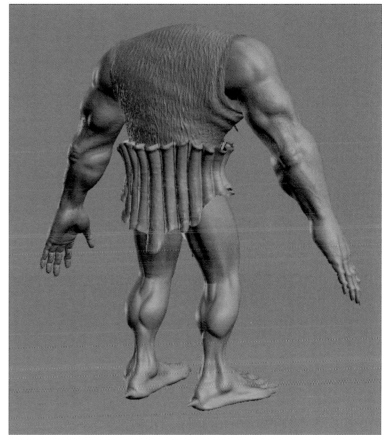

**Figure 7.12** The complete Ogre sculpture.

# 8

# Detail Textures

Textures play a huge role in game development; not only do they add color and depth to your characters, but they also add surface detail to the simplest of geometry. As new graphics cards develop, new shaders are born that allow us artists more freedom with our work—meaning that with textures, we can make up for the limitations of polygons.

Before you begin to build the textures for your Ogre, let's have a look at the current batch of mapping techniques adopted in almost all of today's AAA titles. But first let's acquaint ourselves with shading and surface normals.

## Surface Normals and Shading

Before we delve into the different texture maps, let's look at the fundamental area they affect—the object's surface. Each 3D model has small arrows, called *normals*, which lie on each vertex and face, pointing perpendicular to the component, dictating the direction light should fall from it.

At one time almost all real-time models were rendered using Gouraud Shading, a technique that would light each model on a per-vertex basis, using its normal as a directional guide. The engine would then use basic linear interpolation to work out how the light would affect each polygon by spreading it from vertex to vertex.

As you can see in Figure 8.1, this gave a decent result, but the object would suffer from the light tracing each edge, and on low-resolution models this could highlight each polygon.

Eventually graphics cards brought the ability to calculate lighting on a per-pixel basis rather than per-vertex giving far superior results. As illustrated in Figure 8.1, this allowed lighting to be calculated on each point, using the geometry normals as a guide to help smooth out the light cast across the surface.

This also allows us to tweak the light on each point using one of the texture maps detailed later in this chapter. Depending on the engine and map used, the surface normals could be dictated on a per-pixel basis.

With this in mind, let's move on and take a look at some of the more common detail textures.

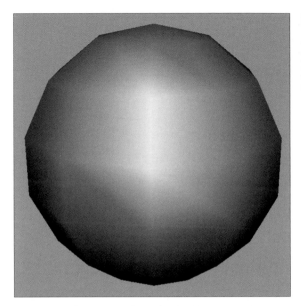

**Figure 8.1**

A sphere with per-vertex and per-pixel lighting.

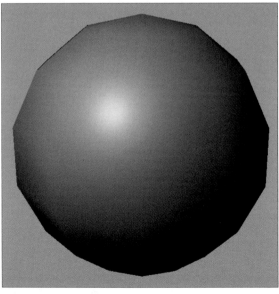

# The Bump Map

Bump mapping is one of the most established techniques for achieving surface detail. Using a basic grayscale texture as a height map, each point on the object's surface would appear to protrude at whiter areas and be recessed at darker pixels. This was, and still is, a quick and easy way to add wrinkles, creases, or simple details to your object because the bump map can be easily hand drawn.

Figure 8.2 shows an example of a surface with and without the bump map texture (from Figure 8.3) applied. As you can see, it is a great way to add basic details to an object.

Because the bump map affects only the surface normals, no geometry is added, and so the object's silhouette remains. Depending on the object itself, this can shatter the illusion that the bump map provides.

# The Normal Map

Also part of the bump map family, the normal map is its younger, more powerful cousin. Instead of relying on a simple grayscale image to dictate height, the normal map is built up of three colors—red, green, and blue—each representing the X, Y, and Z direction of light. This allows the image to store more information on how light should react to the object's surface normals.

So the pale blue pixels are flat areas, pink pixels are normals pointing to the right, and darker blue pixels are pointing left. Green pixels are normals pointing up, and purple pixels are normals pointing down. So you can see how this will produce a better effect, as each pixel is effectively a normal.

You can see an example of a normal map in Figure 8.4 and how it looks applied to a sphere in Figure 8.5.

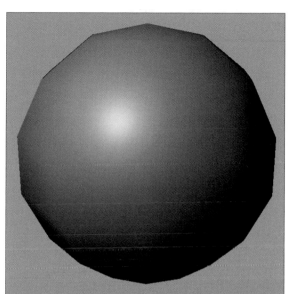

**Figure 8.2**

An object with and without a bump map applied.

**Figure 8.3**

The bump map texture.

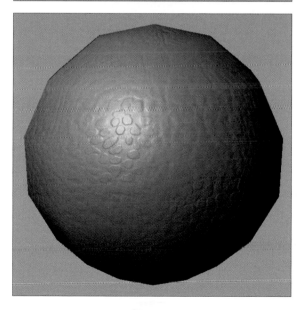

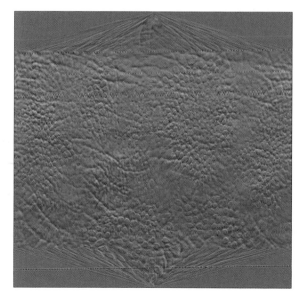

**Figure 8.4**

A normal map.

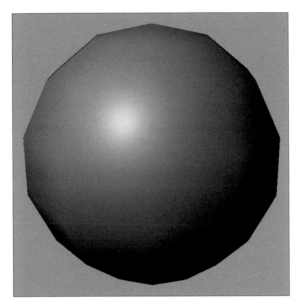

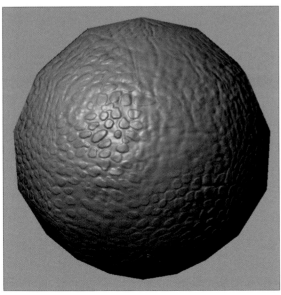

**Figure 8.5**

A sphere with
and without
a normal
map applied.

Because of its nature, the normal map is near impossible to create using a basic painting package. Tools do exist to help convert a simple grayscale image into a normal map, like NVIDIA's Adobe Photoshop plug-in, or Crazy Bump (found on the companion CD) for example, but these should be kept for additional surface detail.

## Crazy Bump

After working my way through this book, I was introduced to Crazy Bump. Soon to be out of beta testing, this excellent application will convert any image into a normal map. Unlike other tools, it does an amazing job and offers many sliders so you can tweak the detail you require in the resulting map. Since discovering it, I have used it countless times to add further detail to my models. I happily recommend you give it a try. In addition to normal maps, it can also generate ambient occlusion and displacement maps.

You will find a special trial version of Crazy Bump on the companion CD.

So how are normal maps generated? Most 3D applications house tools to help you. The user begins, as we have, by creating two models: a high-resolution model (the source) holding the detail needed, and a low-resolution (the target) equivalent. The normal map tool then uses both models, comparing them with each other as it bakes out the differences to a texture.

The resulting image can then be applied back to the target model, adding much welcome detail.

Normal maps generally come in two flavors: object-space and tangent-space (Figure 8.6). Both measure and store the coordinates in different ways, with the information being translated by your game engine; however, tangent-space normal maps are currently used most often in game development.

## The Parallax Map

Taking the normal map one step further is the parallax map. Combining the detail of a normal map with the depth of a height map produces an effect that holds the illusion of true depth or relief when viewed from any angle.

> **Note**
>
> You can simply Google "parallax maps" to find out more information or to find example images.

Let me try and explain how they work. You begin with the normal map, which gives great surface detail but when viewed up close lacks real depth. The parallax code uses the angle of the camera and the height map to offset the object's UV coordinates to give the illusion of depth. As you can imagine, this gives a much better result.

Currently, parallax maps are new to games and can be quite expensive to utilize, but as technology pushes forward, they will become as mainstream as normal maps.

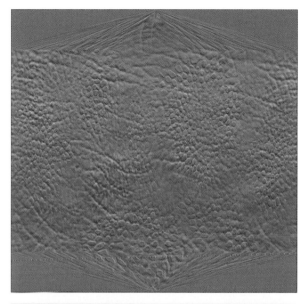

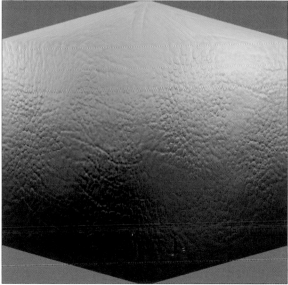

**Figure 8.6** Tangent-space and object-space normal maps.

# The Displacement Map

We are branching away from real-time textures now to investigate a couple other useful texture maps.

Much like a bump map, the displacement map relies on a grayscale image to store its information. This data is then applied to a low-resolution model that is subdivided at render time, allowing the shape to be deformed to fit the detail in the texture map. As you can see in Figure 8.7 (which has the displacement map in Figure 8.8 applied), this results in a high-quality model that is perfect for high-end rendering, but as the resulting surface is a dense mesh, it is no good for the real-time world...at least not yet.

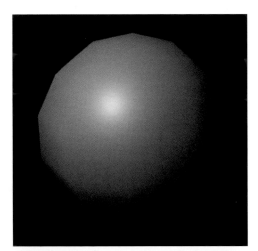

**Figure 8.7**

A displacement map applied to a sphere.

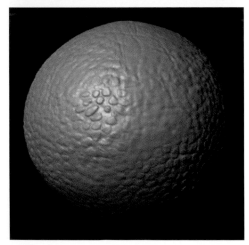

**Figure 8.8**  The displacement map used in Figure 8.7.

# Ambient Occlusion

Finally we have a procedure that is already used in most 3D applications but is slowly moving from the behind the scenes to become a real-time process.

*Ambient occlusion* takes a predefined position, be it the camera or a point above the model, and uses that as a light source. The engine then casts light rays from this point, with each connecting with the model. From this, the ambient occlusion engine can then work out which areas are lit and which are in shadow, and

if needed bakes these out into a texture map. Much like the normal map, this can be done on a high-resolution model, with the texture projected onto a lower-resolution mesh. This can then be used to give the model more depth and ultimately a more realistic look. You can see this applied to our Ogre in Figure 8.9.

As mentioned, ambient occlusion currently isn't used as a real-time process; rather the texture artist can use this process to bake out a light map. This can then be overlaid on top of your texture to provide the depth and lighting needed.

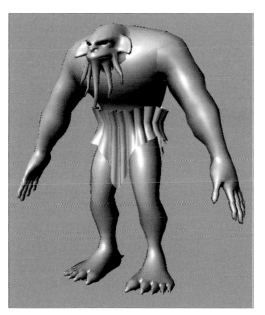 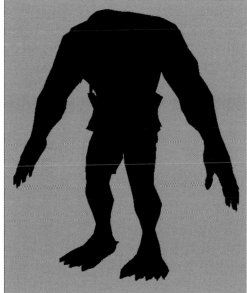 

**Figure 8.9** The Ogre with a flat, ambient occlusion texture applied.

Now that you have a better understanding of each texture technique, I would recommend playing around with your chosen application to discover how these are generated. Bump, normal, and ambient occlusion maps are generally easy to extract, and you will need these later in the book. As for parallax and displacement maps, feel free to skip over these for now.

We now have a choice: we can move on and work on the Ogre's textures, or we can begin building the eyes, belt, hair, and so on. Working on the textures now may be the best bet as it will give us a break from modeling and allow us to look further into detail textures.

# 9

# Texture Building

We can now concentrate on adding color and depth to our Ogre. In this chapter we will paint the base texture before adding detail with the help of textures extracted from our sculpted mesh. Like the sculpting chapter, this will be a general overview of just one process, so feel free to experiment with other techniques.

## Map Extraction

The first thing we should do is pull all the information we will need from our high-resolution model. If you have used Mudbox, ZBrush, or Silo, this will be a simple task since these applications have built in tools for map extraction. The process usually involves having both the source and target models occupying the same space before you use the appropriate tool to extract the normal map. The options when doing this are pretty much the same across packages and allow you to specify a search distance. This distance tells the tool how far outside the target mesh it should look when searching the source model's surface.

As time goes by, these options are being expanded upon to give better and easier results.

First pull the normal maps from the models. Depending on how these are handled you may need to generate a normal map per element before compiling them into a single page. Just remember that you are after two texture pages—one for the body and another for clothing. Your normal maps should look like those in Figure 9.1.

It's a good idea to have a scene setup with which you can test the normal maps to make sure they hold enough detail as well as for checking for errors. This scene can then become the starting block to our final game mesh.

1. To do this, first take the lowest level of each sculpted element and export it as an .obj file.

2. Bring these files into a scene and apply the normal maps to the relevant parts.

3. Now you can see the textures immediately as they would appear in game.

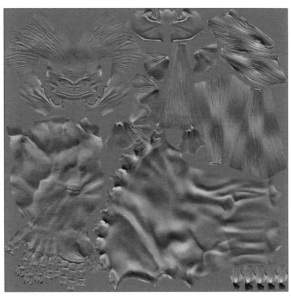

**Figure 9.1**

The extracted normal maps.

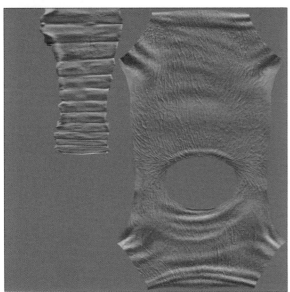

**Note**

If you find that you are ending up with some strange results on the ears or claws, check that the UVs are the correct way around. If they are inverted, the normal map will appear to break through these objects. Simply import the base .obj back into your 3D application, fix the UVs, and send it back into the sculpting package or the application you used to extract the normal map.

With the normal maps applied, and any errors corrected, you should have something similar to that in Figure 9.2. You will be able to see just how much normal maps add to the basic model.

What this also shows us are some nasty angular parts to his silhouette, but don't worry; we will address this in Chapter 10, "Optimization and Refinement."

Next we will need to extract a basic bump map (see Figure 9.3). As mentioned, we will be using the normal map for our surface detail, which should make the bump maps redundant. We will use them instead to add shading and depth to our textures.

Finally, if you are able, bake out the appropriate ambient occlusion maps. These can be tricky to successfully bake and can take a long time to calculate, but they are well worth it. As you can see from Figure 9.4, these images hold vital lighting data that we can overlay onto our color maps to give the character real depth and form.

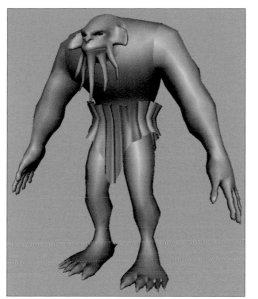
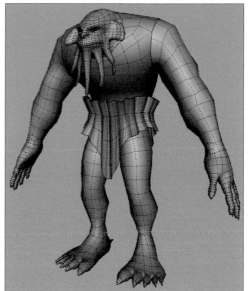
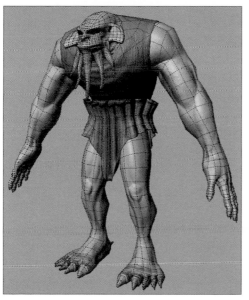

**Figure 9.2**

The extracted normal maps are applied back onto the base mesh, giving amazing results.

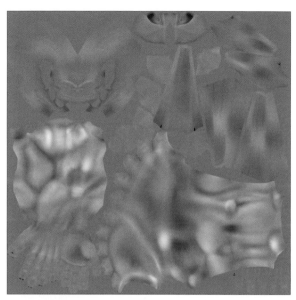

**Figure 9.3**

Extract the bump maps that will help us add shading to our textures.

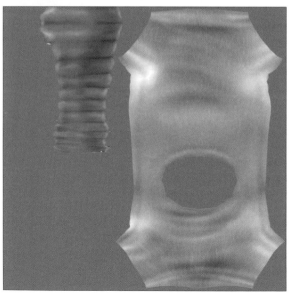

**Figure 9.4**

Finally, bake out the ambient occlusion maps.

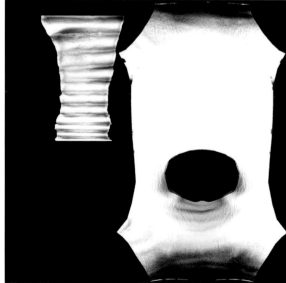

Those are the main maps we will be using—the normal map for surface detail, and the bump and occlusion maps for helping add depth and detail to the color maps that we'll create next.

## Texture Painting

Let's now look at compiling our texture pages. This will first involve the creation of a base-color page (often referred to as a diffuse page) before we use the maps we previously extracted to add further detail.

## Base Colors

To start off our textures, we will need to paint the base colors. This can be approached a couple of ways.

- The traditional way: Exporting a snapshot of your UV layout and then using this as a guide as you paint in your 2D package.

- Using a 3D paint package, you can draw directly onto the 3D model and export the texture to an image file when you are done.

We will look at generating the base texture with the help of a 3D painting package. Not only will this be a quick way to create your texture, but it will also help you to hide the texture seams—a process that would be tricky otherwise, especially around the beard and claws.

Before you begin, you will need something to paint upon, so export the highest level of each element from the sculptured model.

 You can find these elements on the companion CD.

## Head

Let's jump right in and start with the head. We are looking for a basic color layout, so there is no point adding immense amounts of detail at this stage. If needed, we can work in more details once we take the textures into the painting package.

1. Following Figure 9.5, take the head first and bring it into the 3D painting application.

2. Apply a base color—one that resembles the mid-tones on the Ogre's skin.

3. Next work in the hair. Again using a medium color, just follow the lines that are already sculpted. Also begin to block out the beard and the eyebrows.

4. With the base color in place, now use a narrower brush and a slightly darker hair tone to draw darker strands into the hair, beard, and eyebrows.

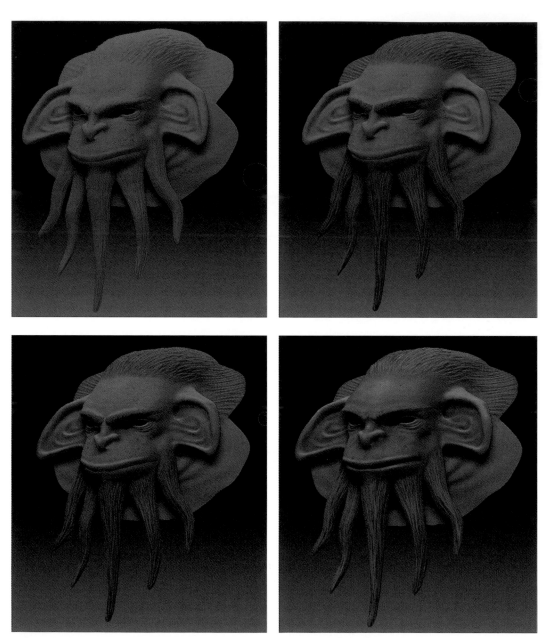

**Figure 9.5**
After applying the base color, work in the subtle shades to help define the face detail.

5. Finally for the hair, repeat the previous step but this time with a lighter color to add highlights.

6. Now move on to the skin. As with the hair, first use a darker shade to deepen the creases and recessed areas.

7. Next work on adding subtle highlights to the wrinkles under his eyes, ears, nose, and lips.

8. To finish, add color to the moles, as well as a slight crimson to his nose, cheeks, and ears.

This should be enough color for now (see Figure 9.6); once extracted and applied to our low-poly model, this should give us a good starting point.

**Figure 9.6** A close-up of the Ogre's face.

## Arm and Hand

Let's move on to the arm next. You can follow the progress in Figure 9.7.

1. Import the high-resolution arm model into your chosen 3D painting application.

2. Apply the same base color as you did with the head.

3. Using a darker shade, trace the lines of the muscles with a thick, soft brush, smoothing each stroke afterward. This will help to define the muscles while varying the skin tones.

4. Next work on the hand, adding shading to the knuckles as well as applying a lighter cream color to the finger nails.

5. Continue to add details like hair on his arm and a pale blue to the veins, as well as adding more veins to the upper and lower hand.

## Leg and Foot

The last of the fleshy parts is the leg. This will be approached in a similar way to the arm, and you can see its progress in Figure 9.8.

1. After importing the leg mesh, apply the base color.

2. Add a cream color to the claws next, to help differentiate them from the skin.

3. Finally add darker and lighter tones to help bring out the muscles and add variation to the skin tones.

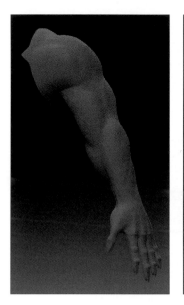

**Figure 9.7**

Bring in the arm mesh and work in the different skin and shading tones.

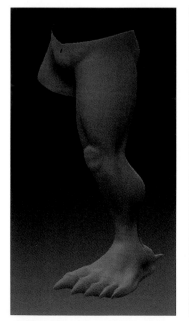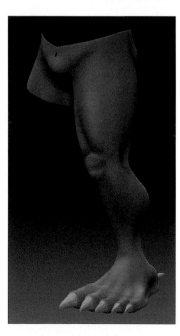

**Figure 9.8**

Next work on the leg, adding different shades to add depth to the muscles, and vary the skin color.

# Clothing

The final parts to paint are the Ogre's clothing. These are quite easy to apply color to, as initially we just need to enhance the creases and folds. As you can see with the shirt (Figure 9.9), after you have added the base color, you lighten the upper folds while darkening the recesses beneath. After this you simply add light and dark strokes to help bring out the fur texture.

Moving on to the loin cloth, we first work with the folds, applying a darker tone between each fold with a contrasting, lighter color on the top. Next we simply lighten the upper and lower seams before adding texture to the material (see Figure 9.10).

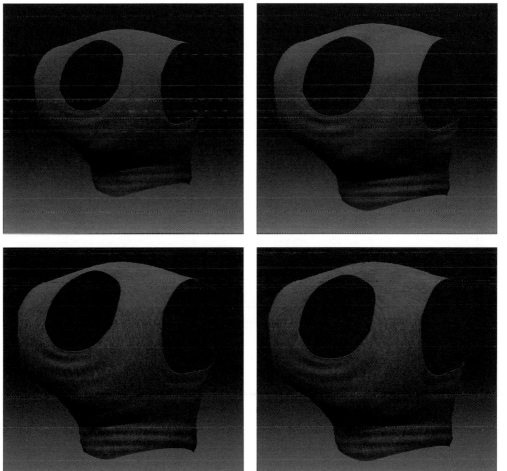

**Figure 9.9**

With the shirt, first enhance the folds before adding detail to the fur.

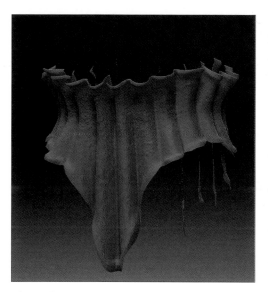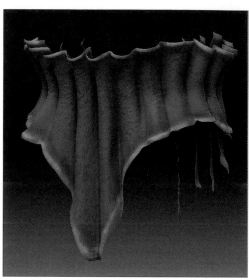

**Figure 9.10**  Again, enhancing the folds is important when working with the loin cloth.

We are more or less finished with the base color textures. Before moving on to the next stage, feel free to work further on these textures and add in more detail if you so desire.

# Compiling

We almost have our main texture pages ready to be compiled. Before we move on, you will need to export the textures you painted in the previous section. As with the normal maps, these may then need putting together onto two pages, like the ones in Figure 9.11, before we proceed.

Let's take a moment now to see how our color maps look on our base model, with the normal map also applied. Figure 9.12 shows our base mesh with default lighting, the model with the color maps applied in a scene with both no lighting and default lighting, and finally the combination of color, normal map, and default lighting. Our Ogre is really starting to take shape.

| Tip |
| --- |
| It's important not to rely too much on the normal map to add detail to your model. It's a good idea to work on the base texture in an unlit scene, getting it nice and detailed before you view it with the normal map. At the end of the day, normal maps serve only to add lighting detail to the model; the diffuse texture is still the crucial element. |

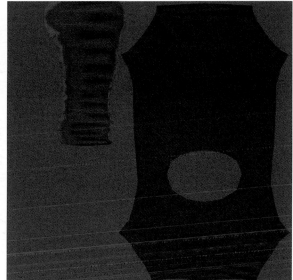

**Figure 9.11**

The exported and compiled base color pages.

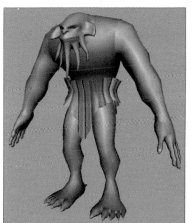

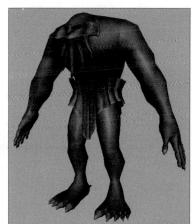

**Figure 9.12** The base mesh with the color and normal map textures applied.

Next we will bring our textures together, using the detail and lighting information in the bump and occlusion maps to enhance our model.

1. Following Figure 9.13, take the base color map for the body into a 2D painting application, preferably one that works with layers.

2. Bring in the bump map first and use an Overlay filter on the layer (if one is available). What you should see is that the bump map has added to the color map, exactly matching the light and dark areas to help bring them out of the image.

3. The effect of the bump map will more than likely be too strong, so lower the opacity of the layer to around 50 percent.

4. Finally, bring in the ambient occlusion map. Again, use an Overlay filter so this is added to the previous layers.

5. You should now see a dramatic change as shadows are added, but they will probably be too dark, so adjust this layer's opacity to around 50 percent too.

Repeat this process with our second texture page so you end up with something resembling Figure 9.14.

With this lighting pass complete, let's have a look at how it has affected our model. If you look at the comparison in Figure 9.15, you can see a dramatic difference. The surface has much more contrast, with the shadows adding much-needed depth to the character.

This is a great start to our Ogre, and for now we will leave him as is. We'll return to his textures in the next chapter when we have added the remaining objects needed and can see him as a whole.

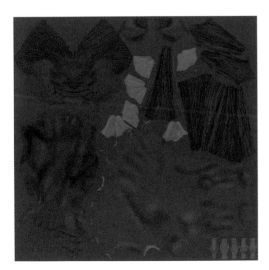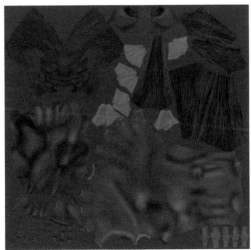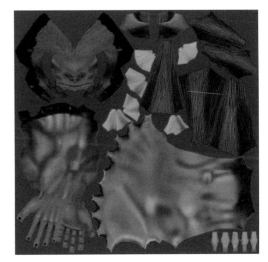

**Figure 9.13** Using the bump map and ambient occlusion maps, you can add vital lighting detail.

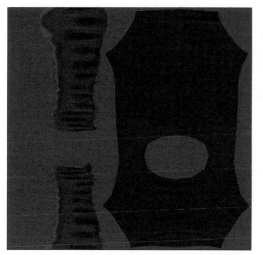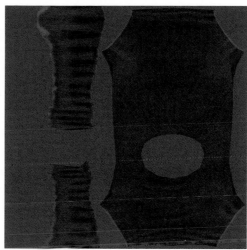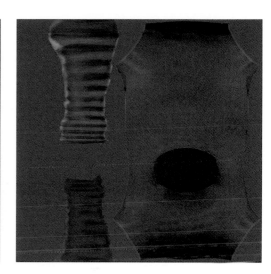

**Figure 9.14** Follow the steps again, this time for the second texture page.

**Figure 9.15**

A comparison of the Ogre before and after the lighting maps were added.

# Specular Maps

Before ending this chapter, we need to address one more texture map. The *specular map* (or gloss map) is traditionally a grayscale image that dictates the glossy and matte areas on a character. Whiter areas are shinier and darker areas dull, meaning we can easily give the skin and clothing the correct appearance.

Figure 9.16 shows the initial specular maps for the Ogre; notice how they are quite dark apart from areas like the claws, eyes, and lips. Although skin can appear flat, it does have a subtle shine to it due to its oiliness, so we need a slight highlight. The lips and claws will need to appear glossier, so they are whiter on the page.

Figure 9.17 shows these maps applied to the creature. First we enable the gloss texture, which makes him appear plastic, but once we apply the textures, the effect is toned down.

In addition to this sort of specular map (often referred to as a specular power map), you may also need a specular color map. The specular power map controls the intensity of the highlight; the specular color map dictates its color. Figure 9.18 shows an example of a combined specular power and color map.

As you can see in Figure 9.19, this gives an extra tint to the character, which offers more depth to the colors.

This stage of the texturing is now complete, but our character is still a long way from being finished. In the next chapter we will create the missing pieces and add extra hair and fur, and frayed edges to his sleeves.

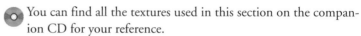 You can find all the textures used in this section on the companion CD for your reference.

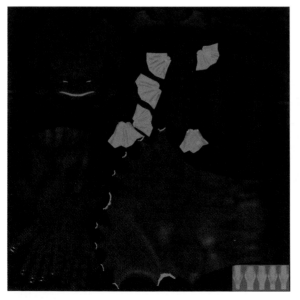

**Figure 9.16**

The initial specular maps for the Ogre.

**Figure 9.17**

The specular map applied to the Ogre.

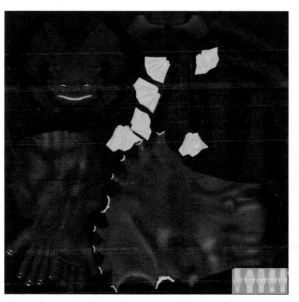
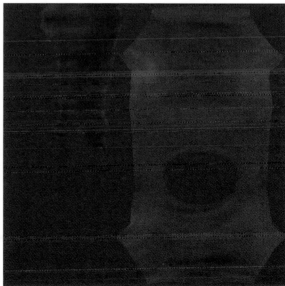

**Figure 9.18**

Combined specular power and color maps.

**Figure 9.19**

The Ogre with
the specular
color map
applied.

# 10

# Optimization and Refinement

At this stage you should be looking at a good base model, minus a few obvious pieces. Before we move on and add the eyes, fur, and other accessories, we will take a look at our character and work on smoothing out some of the jagged areas of its silhouette while also taking the opportunity to remove any polygons we simply don't need.

We are doing this now because the overall shape of the Ogre will change during the course of this chapter, meaning if we had previously added the fur, for example, we would need to reposition it.

## Silhouette Refinement

Without even turning the lighting off in the scene, we can see some angular areas around our Ogre, mainly on the arms and legs. In this section we will focus on smoothing out the limbs to make them more organic, and less "gamelike."

Let's look at what we have. In Figure 10.1 you can see our current model, both lit and unlit to help emphasize the silhouette. Initially, as mentioned, you can see some sharp, polygonal lines on the upper arms and calves, so let's tackle these first.

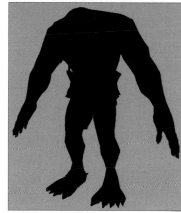

**Figure 10.1** Looking at the Ogre without lighting will help to highlight the angular areas of its silhouette.

Luckily the limbs are mirrored, which will save us doing twice the work. Let's look at the arm first.

1. Begin by hiding all the other elements so you are left with just one arm. Rotating around it, you will see that the upper arm needs some more polygons added to smooth the muscles.

2. Following Figure 10.2, first insert edge loops around the upper arm and elbow, splitting the larger polygons.

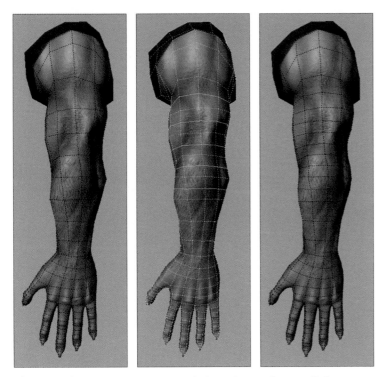

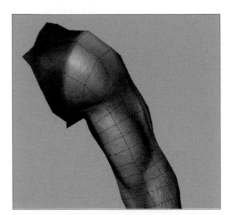

Figure 10.3

Next divide the shoulder and smooth the harsh curve.

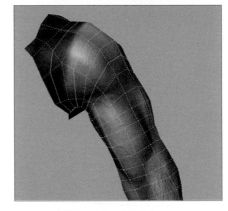

**Figure 10.2** Divide the upper arm before relaxing the overall shape.

3. Next refine the shape to take advantage of the new topology. If you have one, try using a "Relax" tool to soften the shape.

4. Now move to the shoulder (Figure 10.3).

5. As you can see, this is quite a harsh joint. This is also a key deforming area and so will need more geometry added to keep it smooth as it bends, so insert a couple of edge loops around the main sections.

6. Finally, as with the upper arm, relax the overall shape to smooth the shoulder.

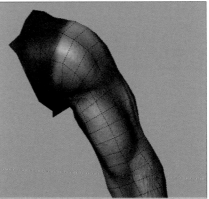

That's the arm nicely smoothed. The rest of the limb is fine for our needs, so let's move on to the leg.

1. Following Figure 10.4, hide the arm and bring in the leg.

2. We will repeat the process we adopted on the arm, so initially divide the polygons around the areas we need to smooth—i.e., the calves, knee, and thigh.

3. Use the new vertices to fill out the shape and reduce the angles.

4. Pan down and zoom in on the foot so you have a view similar to that in Figure 10.5.

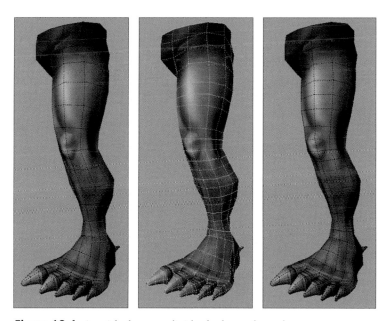

**Figure 10.4** As with the arm, divide the leg and use the new geometry to smooth out the harsh edges.

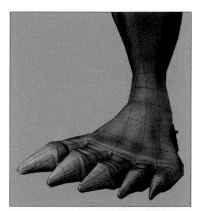

**Figure 10.5**

To complete the leg, smooth out the claws.

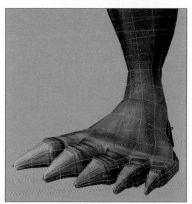

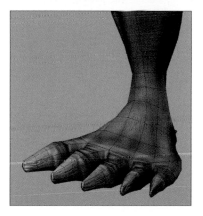

5. At present the claws look OK, but from a distance they look boxy. Add two edge loops cutting around the foot and across each claw.

6. Relaxing the general area softens both the foot and the claws.

That's the key areas smoothed, meaning we have softened the harsh silhouette of the Ogre. You can see before and after shots of this in Figure 10.6.

Quickly check the rest of the model to see if you can find any more areas that could benefit from additional geometry, but the work you have done here should be sufficient as you've covered the obvious areas that needed attention.

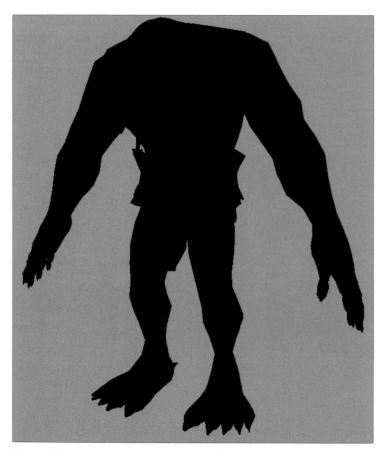

**Figure 10.6** The Ogre before and after the smoothing process.

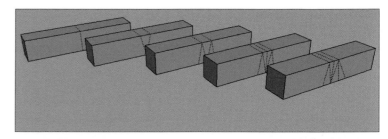

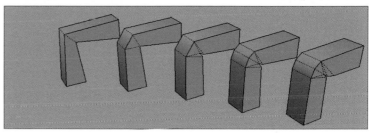

**Figure 10.7** As you can see, having a few more polygons can help to retain the volume of the deforming box.

> **Note**
>
> Try not to add geometry unless you feel it is necessary. Remember that when you are working with a strict budget, you may end up being told to remove the polygons after you have added them.

# Optimization and Deformation

Now that we have added geometry to help soften the shape of our Ogre, it's time to remove some to balance things out. In this section we will both optimize the model and work on key deforming areas to help them bend successfully.

## Bend but Don't Break

It's important to look at game characters and how they bend and deform. What you need to consider is how key areas—like the elbows, knees, and fingers—look as they bend to extremes. The topology needs to be constructed so that as the elbow, for example, rotates, the inner and outer elbow don't pinch badly or look rough and angular.

Take a look at Figure 10.7. This shows examples of different bend configurations and highlights the need for the correct topology. The first box pinches badly when bent, but the last one retains its shape because of the extra geometry.

As you work around the Ogre, keep this in mind to ensure good deformation when the time comes to rig and animate him.

With a good idea of how our main joints topology should look, let's continue this section and look at optimization.

> **Tip**
>
> If you have time, try throwing a couple of joints/bones into your model just to test the deforming areas before you finalize them

## Polygon Culling

When working with game models, be they characters, vehicles, or environment props, you have to learn to be economical. Even as game consoles grow ever more powerful, it's still important to stick to budgets, and where possible work well within them.

To help with this, and our model, let's look at what polygons are safe to remove. These can be broken down into two main sections, *unwanted polygons* and *unused polygons*.

## Unwanted Polygons

Unwanted geometry is simply areas that are hidden and are never seen in the game. Take the example in Figure 10.8: The character has complete spheres for her eyes, yet the backs of them will never be seen, so they are effectively a waste of resources.

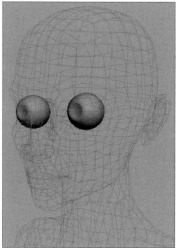

**Figure 10.8**  This sort of model doesn't need full spheres for the eyes, so the backs of the eyes are unwanted polygons.

Other examples could include backpacks, belts, or any accessory that lies on the surface of the character. If it has polygons on the side facing the character, make sure they will be easily seen; if not, get rid of them!

## Unused Polygons

Unused polygons are those which can be seen but do not add to the shape of the model, or add to it in such a subtle way that they would not be missed if removed.

Look at the cubes in Figure 10.9; they are identical in every way except in topology. Switching on their wire-frame reveals that the second holds many more polygons that do not add to the shape—so, they can be discarded.

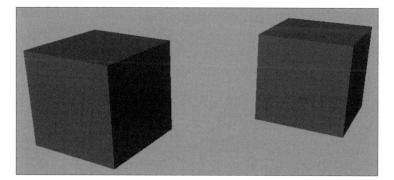

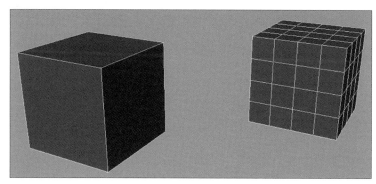

**Figure 10.9**  The second cube has more geometry, but it doesn't add to the overall shape, so the extra polygons can be discarded.

The example in Figure 10.10 shows two boxes, but one has a slight bulge in its center. The bulge is so subtle that if we removed it, no one would be able to tell, especially if this were a finger on a character running around the screen.

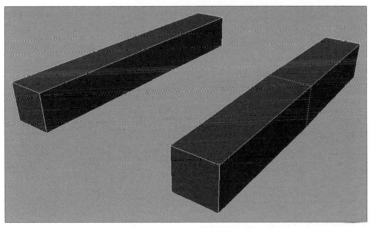

**Figure 10.10** The bulge in the second box is so subtle that no one would miss it if we removed it.

I hope from this brief section you have gained a small understanding of the areas we will be looking at next as we begin to optimize our Ogre.

## Off to Work

It's time to start working again. To make things a little easier, we will examine each piece of the Ogre separately, so load in your model and let's begin.

### Head

We will start with the head, but you have to be careful what you remove. The face is usually created in such a way that it needs extra geometry so it can animate successfully. The mouth and eyes, for example, have a few edge loops around them that we could happily reduce, but these may be needed to enable better lip syncing and facial expressions.

If you're not sure, the best thing to do would be to ask an animator.

So, Figure 10.11 shows our current head. We will reduce the mouth area first.

1. The edge ring highlighted in Figure 10.12, running across the top of the mouth and down the beard, can be collapsed since it doesn't add too much to the shape, nor will it help with facial animation.

2. Moving to the top of the head, now we can see that there is quite a lot of geometry up here. In the next chapter we will add hair that will cover most of his scalp, so we can afford to lose some of these polygons.

3. Following Figure 10.13, first select the ring of edges on either side of the center. We don't collapse the ones in the exact center; depending on your model, this may cause UV problems.

**Figure 10.11**

The current unoptimized head.

**Figure 10.12**

Removing the edge loop above the lip will not cause any problems.

 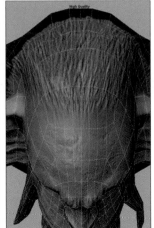 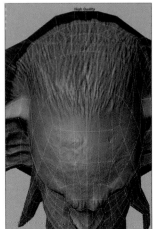 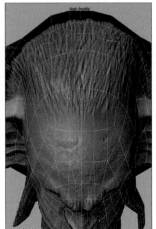 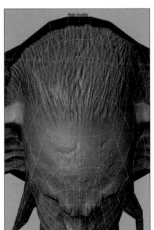

**Figure 10.13**  Collapsing the edges on either side of the scalp will reduce the polygons and leave a cleaner-looking model.

4. Once you have collapsed those, select the resulting edges on either side.

5. Collapsing these will leave a cleaner-looking scalp.

Now that we have reduced the top of the head, the brow looks crowded, and we also have an odd-looking polygon across the eyebrow.

1. As shown in Figure 10.14, select the middle row of edges running back from the eyebrow.

**Figure 10.14** Reduce the polygons around the brow area to even out the flow of polygons.

2. Collapse these to even out the brow area.

3. Now we can address the polygon at the front of the eyebrow. As it stands, the topology here makes the eyebrow appear concave and unnatural. A simple cut bridging the vertices on either side, as in Figure 10.15, will fix this. Be sure to delete the old vertical edge too if it still exists, as this will pull the new edge back.

**Figure 10.15** Create a cut across the concave polygon on the eyebrows.

There are quite a few polygons hiding beneath the head that we can remove. These are behind the beard and under the chin, adding nothing to the overall shape.

1. Select the edge ring highlighted in Figure 10.16. It should run down either side of the central beard and up onto the chin.

2. As you can see, collapsing these has made little difference to the shape, and this area may not be seen often, so it's a safe sacrifice.

**Figure 10.16** Select and collapse the unused polygons behind the beard and beneath the chin.

3. Now that we have altered the back of the beard, let's look at the front, which has the same topology (Figure 10.17).

4. A quick glance at the front shows us that we can easily reduce it in the same way with little change.

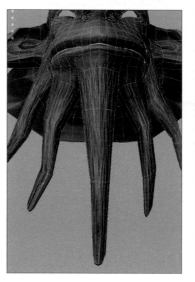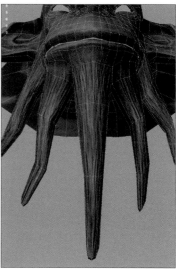

**Figure 10.17** Reduce the front of the beard.

Rotate around the model now and see if any other areas stand out. Look for unneeded polygons and edges that can be collapsed.

---

**Tip**

If you are unsure how something will look, trust in the good old "Undo" command. Collapse the edges, and if you are not happy, just undo the action.

**Note**

Be careful when collapsing edges along UV seams and if possible avoid it altogether. Reducing in the wrong area will cause the texture to tear and any seamless areas to break.

The ears look like good candidates for optimization. The front and back are only slightly curved, so let's see if we can squeeze some polygons out of them.

1. Switch to a front-on perspective and select the upper middle row of edges, as illustrated in Figure 10.18.

2. As you collapse these, you may see the texture jump slightly, but don't worry; so long as the ears still look OK, we are good to go.

3. Next select the lower three vertical edges and collapse those.

4. Move around behind the ears now and select the upper middle edge ring as shown in Figure 10.19. Don't be afraid to follow this ring to the edge of the head if the resulting shape is satisfactory.

5. Once collapsed, move to the lower middle edge ring and collapse that.

**Note**

You may have noticed that we didn't alter the outer edges of the ears. This was to help preserve the silhouette. Reducing the inner faces works because on the ears you will never see the polygons, but keeping the outer edges will keep the illusion of the model being smooth.

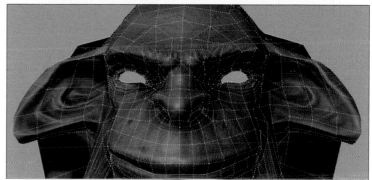
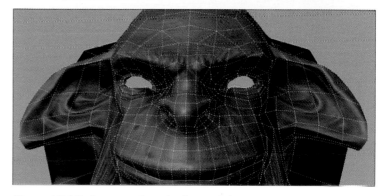

**Figure 10.18** Start to reduce the front of the ears.

**Figure 10.19** Next work on the back of each ear.

Moving around the model again, we can see some polygons to reduce in the lower neck area. This section will be hidden by both the beard and the shirt, so we can reduce it without worrying.

1. Looking from beneath the head, select the edges highlighted in Figure 10.20—the ones on either side of the neck.

2. Once collapsed, the neck should still look OK.

One of the last areas we will reduce will be the outer sections of his beard. Looking from behind them (Figure 10.21), we can see there are quite a few polygons that more than likely won't be seen.

Looking from beneath, select the middle, vertical edge ring of the outer beard sections, and collapse them.

That's the head pretty much complete, but as always you could probably work on it further. Spend some time now looking around to see if you can find any more areas to optimize or clean up.

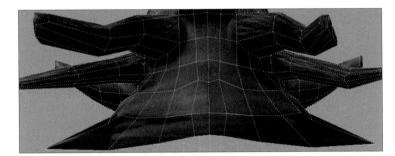

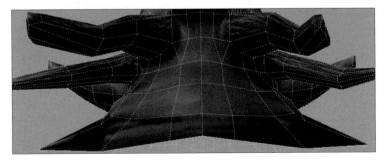

**Figure 10.20** The neck will more than likely be hidden, so you can safely reduce it further.

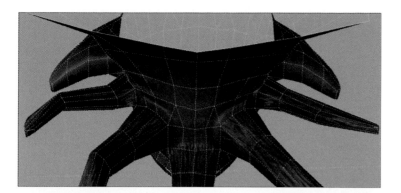

**Figure 10.22**

Bringing back the torso shows us that much of the outer head is hidden.

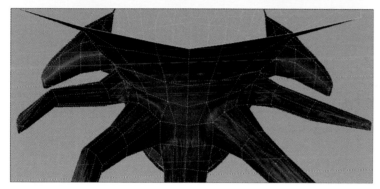

**Figure 10.21** Finally, reduce the back of the outer sections of beard.

Before we move on, there is one more section we can address. If you look at Figure 10.22, when we bring back the shirt, we can see it covers most of the outer sections of the head. The clavicle and shoulder areas are hidden and therefore are not needed.

Looking from inside the torso will help us to determine which areas we can delete. Following Figure 10.23, work your way around the outer edges, collapsing them one by one while making sure the view from outside remains the same. Removing too much will leave a hole around the neck line.

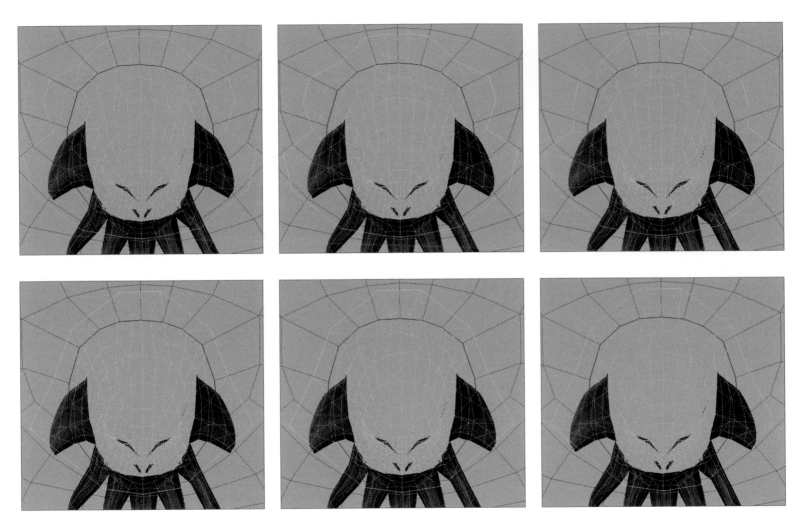

**Figure 10.23** Work on the inner parts of the head to reduce areas that will not be seen.

## Torso and Loin Cloth

Working our way down brings us to the clothing. Judging from Figure 10.24, there isn't going to be much optimizing needed for these.

These are clean models with enough polygons to enable them to deform without problems. What we can do, though, is insert an edge loop around the shoulders to help with deformation in this key area. This will also add an indentation where the straps around the arm will go.

1. Focus on the left shoulder and create an edge loop running just inside the opening (see Figure 10.25).

2. Adding this cut has produced a five-sided polygon. At this stage this isn't really a problem, but to keep things clean, collapse the outer edge to return it to a quad.

3. Make sure textures are enabled and adjust the vertices of the new cut (see Figure 10.26), pulling them inward to create a crease. It's a good idea to have the arms visible for this, just so you know you aren't moving the components too far.

4. Finally, repeat this process on the right shoulder, and you are done.

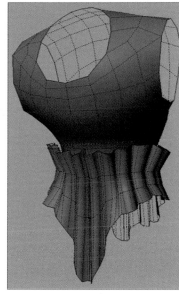

**Figure 10.24** Looking at the clothing, there isn't much optimization needed.

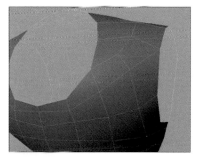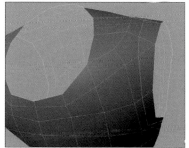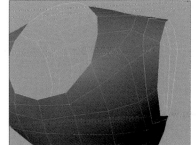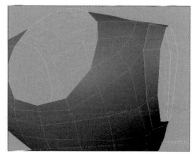

**Figure 10.25** Create an edge loop just inside the shoulder opening.

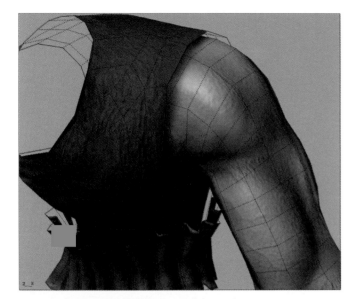

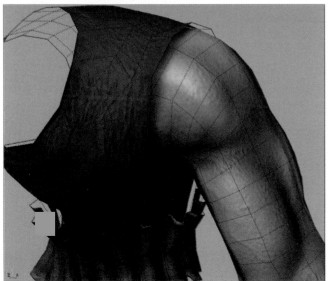

**Figure 10.26** With the arm and textures visible, tweak the new vertices to create the crease.

Now, looking at the torso as a whole, you can see the added sleeves have given his shirt some much-needed detail (see Figure 10.27), and we can use the cuts to guide the placement of the straps in the next chapter.

**Figure 10.27** The added creases help give the shirt more detail.

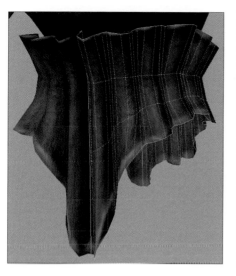 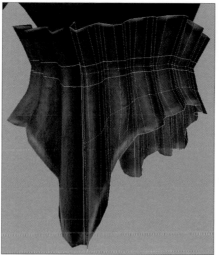 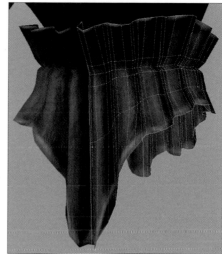

**Figure 10.28**
Create two edge loops around the loin cloth and scale the middle one to create the crease.

What we have just done for the sleeves we can now do for the loin cloth. Eventually we will be adding a belt, so to help us later, and to add detail to the cloth, we will create a crease.

1. The loin cloth is currently mirrored, meaning we only need to work on one side, so, as illustrated in Figure 10.28, focus on the left side.

2. Create two edge loops running around the cloth, one above the upper middle row and one below it.

3. Now scale the edge loop in between the two new ones inward to create the crease.

That is probably enough work on the clothing for now. As you can see from Figure 10.29, we have made some subtle changes, but changes that have improved the overall shape.

**Figure 10.29** With the creases created, we have added subtle detail to the model.

## Arm and Hand

Now things are going to get interesting as we move on to the arm and hand or, to be exact, the fingers. Figure 10.30 shows the current arm model.

We added quite a bit of geometry earlier to smooth out the muscle tone, but now we need to rework some of that and try and chop some of it out while retaining the shape.

1. Turn to Figure 10.31 and focus on the shoulder. We added edge loops to help smooth the deltoid, which worked nicely but has left us with more geometry than we need in the armpit.

2. Select the edges at the front and follow them under the arm. Don't continue over the top of the shoulder because we want to keep these polygons.

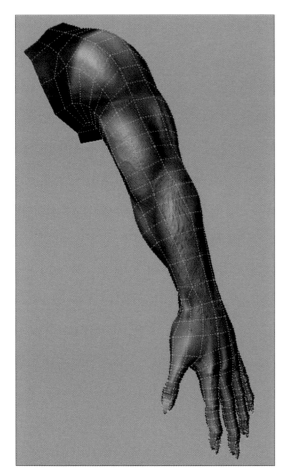

**Figure 10.30** The current arm model.

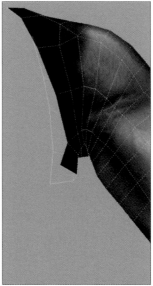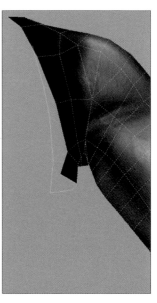

**Figure 10.31** Start to remove the polygons at the front of the shoulder and armpit.

3. Collapse these edges. What we have now is the best of both worlds—more geometry over the top of the shoulder to account for the curve but no excess polygons below.

4. Turn to the back of the shoulder now and repeat the process; you can follow this in Figure 10.32.

5. Select the two edges at the back of the shoulder and follow them under the arm.

6. Collapse these edges to clean up the armpit.

7. Before we move on, there is more we can do in this area. Move under the arm so you are looking up at the armpit (see Figure 10.33).

8. There is a ring of small polygons. These do add to the shape, but if we try and remove them, we will see that they will not be missed.

Moving down the arm, we can take a look at the next joint, the elbow. We need to make sure that if we remove any geometry from this area, it will still bend successfully.

As Figure 10.34 illustrates, we can remove the polygons from the front of the elbow, but we don't want to remove them from the rear.

Figure 10.35 shows the back. We left the polygons intact to cope with the bend.

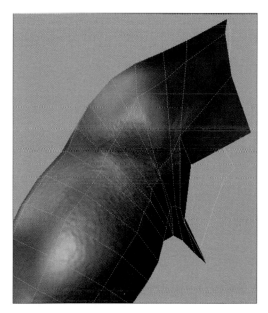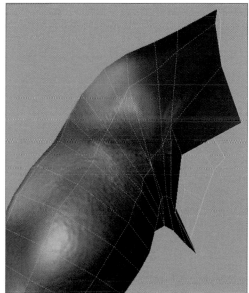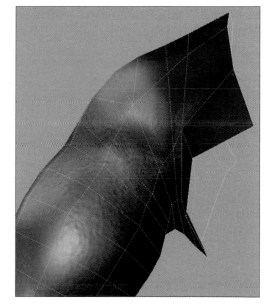

**Figure 10.32** Continue to the back of the shoulder, removing the excess polygons.

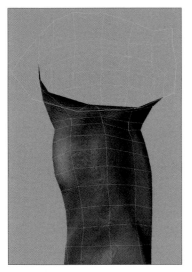 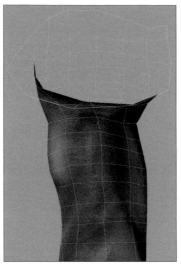

**Figure 10.33** We can also remove this small ring of polygons; they will not be missed.

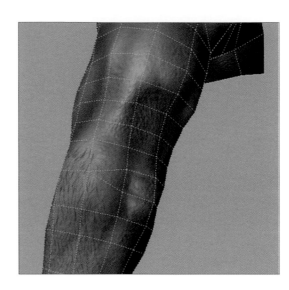

**Figure 10.35**
Leave the polygons at the back to help with deformation.

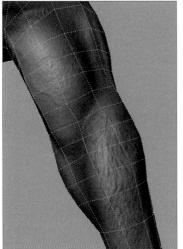 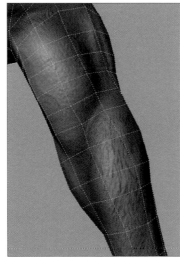

**Figure 10.34** Moving to the elbow, we can collapse the edges at the front of the arm.

We can now do something similar farther down the arm. Take a look at Figure 10.36. The silhouette on the top of the forearm is more or less flat, but beneath it we have a curve.

If you collapse the edges across the top, the resulting shape is almost the same. We have chopped out some geometry while also keeping the curve under the arm.

Moving back to the elbow, we have been left with a large polygon. When this area bends, it will start to look angular, so we need to add some polygons back in. To do this, we don't want to just insert another edge loop, because this will split the faces all the way around the arm. Instead we can create a cut from the upper pivot of the elbow around to the lower one (see Figure 10.37).

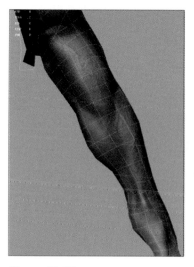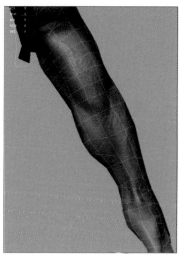

**Figure 10.36** Collapsing the edges on top of the forearm will leave the curve underneath.

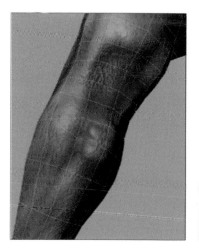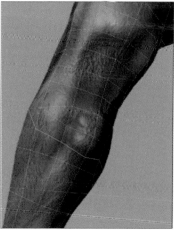

**Figure 10.37** Create a cut from the upper pivot of the elbow to the lower to help soften the joint when it bends.

The final area on the upper arm is just under the arm. If you look at Figure 10.38, you will notice that the area beneath the arm is almost flat. This means we can easily remove some polygons and it will still look the same.

1. First select the three vertical edges running down the middle of the flat area.

2. Collapsing these will highlight another area we can optimize.

3. Select the edges below the ones you just collapsed.

4. Removing these may look drastic, but overall the area's silhouette looks almost the same.

The main arm has been optimized and refined. We can now look at reducing the excess geometry hidden beneath the shirt.

1. Bring back the shirt and move your camera so you are inside, looking at the arm, in a view similar to that in Figure 10.39.

2. Straight away we can see some redundant polygons. These are on the corners, clearly not adding to the arm or visible from the outside. Select the edges shown in Figure 10.39 and collapse them.

3. Next remove the ring across the top, but be careful that from the outside the arm still looks full. What I mean by this is that there are no obvious holes when looking at the shoulder. We need to maintain the illusion that the upper body exists and is hidden beneath the shirt.

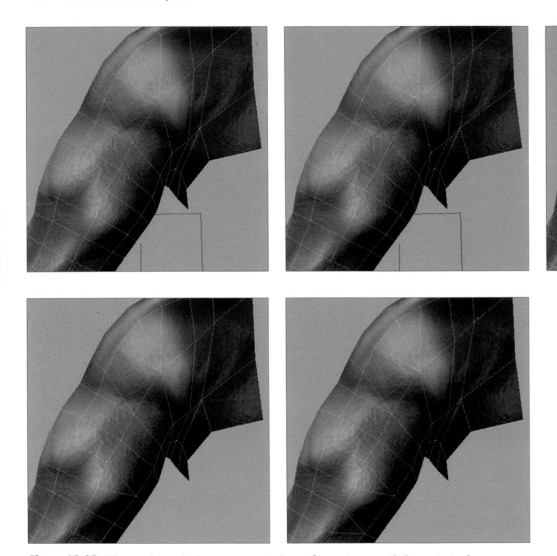

**Figure 10.38** The area beneath the upper arm is almost flat, so it can easily be optimized.

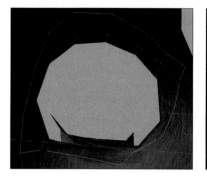 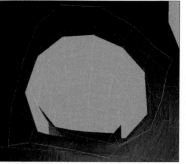 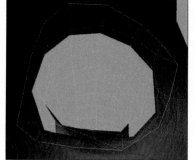 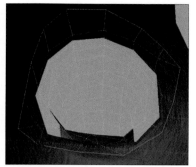

**Figure 10.39** Remove the redundant polygons hidden beneath the shirt.

We are finished with the main arm, for now, so let's move down and take a look at the hand and fingers. The hand looks OK at the moment, but we can do more with it. First of all, the joints need to be adjusted so the fingers will bend properly, and while we are doing this, we can address the other issue of the knuckles lacking definition.

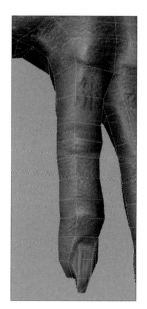 

**Figure 10.40**

Create two cuts across the top of the knuckle.

1. As illustrated in Figure 10.40, focus on the first knuckle of the index finger.

2. Create two cuts around the knuckle, ending them at the pivot for the joint.

3. Move around to behind the knuckle (see Figure 10.41) and create similar cuts. This extra geometry will be essential in keeping the fingers from pinching when they bend.

4. Now that we have these new vertices, we might as well make them work. Pan around to the side of the finger and adjust them to smooth out the shape of the knuckle (see Figure 10.42).

 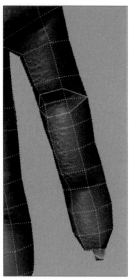

**Figure 10.41**

Add similar cuts to the rear of the knuckle.

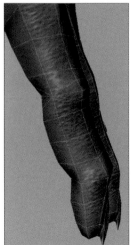 

**Figure 10.42**

Adjust the new vertices to fill out the shape of the knuckle.

5. Finally, if you feel that there may be more polygons than you need in this area, you can collapse the upper ones shown in Figure 10.43. I would recommend, however, leaving the polygons below the knuckle.

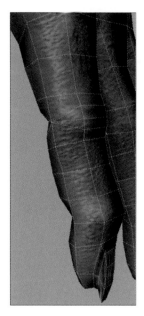 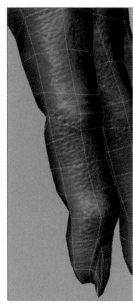

**Figure 10.43**

If needed, you can collapse the upper edges, but leave the lower ones.

That's one knuckle complete. Now start to work your way through the hand, applying the same procedure to the rest of the fingers.

One problem you may face as you do this is the edges not aligning with the knuckles or creases. Take a look at Figure 10.44. If you look at the middle finger, you will notice the creases behind the knuckles don't lie on the polygon edges. In order for the finger to bend believably, we need the crease to be on an edge.

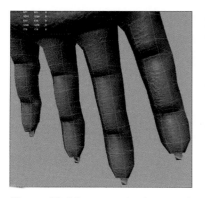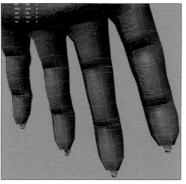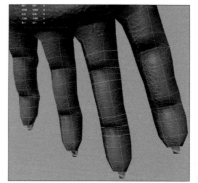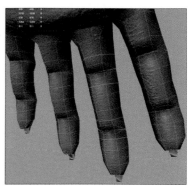

**Figure 10.44** Insert edge loops to help keep the knuckle crease on edges.

Let's fix this problem.

1. Following Figure 10.44, first create two edge loops, making sure these follow the creases.

2. Next create four more edge loops outside the neighboring ones.

3. Using these new loops, you can start to construct the shapes we need for the knuckles while ensuring that they lie in exactly the same place as dictated by the texture.

Figure 10.45 illustrates what the Ogre's hand should now look like. Each finger has more definition and will deform well.

There is one more section we need to address before moving on to the leg. As you can see from Figure 10.46, the point where the fingers meet the hand is currently lacking in topology. This might mean that as the fingers bend, the knuckle might collapse or pinch. Simply create an edge loop across these polygons, making sure to smooth and optimize the area when done.

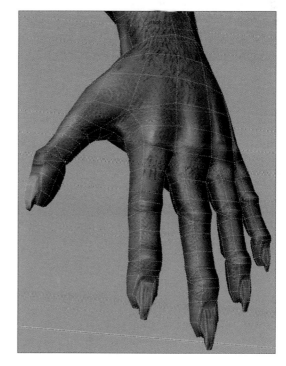

**Figure 10.45**

The finished fingers with extra definition.

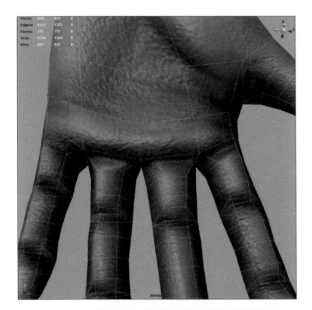

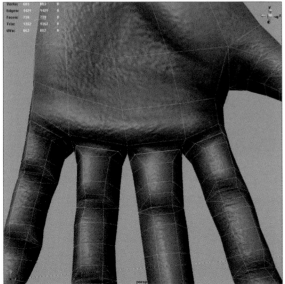

**Figure 10.46** Adding edge loops where the hand meets the fingers will help the fingers bend.

So that's the arm complete. Looking at Figure 10.47, we now have a smooth, well-defined arm with workable joints.

Before we move on, look at Figure 10.48 and see what we have done so far.

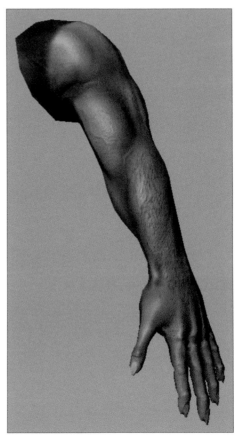

**Figure 10.47**

The final, optimized, and refined arm.

**Figure 10.48** Your work so far.

## Leg

In this last section of the chapter, we'll optimize the leg. Figure 10.49 shows the current leg model. On first glance it seems fine; there are enough polygons to help define the silhouette while also helping when deforming, but let's look closer and see what we can do.

If you focus on the thigh, it's smooth with no obvious places to optimize until you look at the inner thigh. This area is pretty much straight, so we can afford to lose an edge ring. Select the ring highlighted in Figure 10.50 and collapse it.

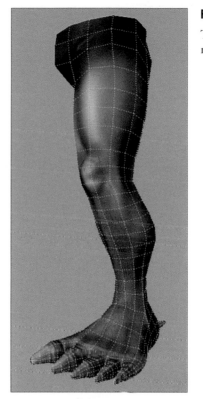

**Figure 10.49**
The current leg model.

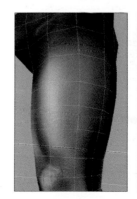

**Figure 10.50** You can afford to remove the central, horizontal edge ring.

Removing this has altered the shape slightly, but it will never be noticed.

Focus on the knee now (see Figure 10.51). The rear of the knee has enough geometry to cope with deforming, but the front is lacking, meaning when bent, it will become jagged.

1. Following Figure 10.51, create an edge loop just below the knee.

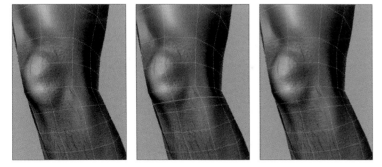

**Figure 10.51** Add an edge loop below the knee to help deformation.

2. Turning to the side now, we will remove the unwanted faces from the rear. Select the edges shown in Figure 10.52, making sure not to go all around the knee.

3. Collapsing these brings the back of the knee back to its original state while retaining the extra geometry needed at the front.

4. All that is left to do now is refine the knee cap, using the extra geometry to smooth out the shape and add definition. You can see an example of this in Figure 10.53.

Moving down, we come to the shin and calf area. Figure 10.54 shows us that while the calf is curved and needs the geometry, the shin is almost flat, so this is the area we can optimize.

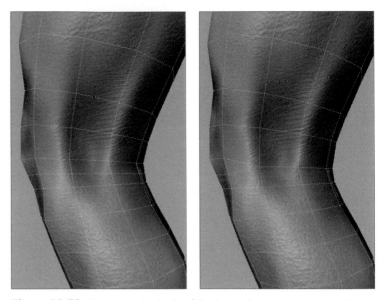

**Figure 10.52** Optimize the back of the knee; the new geometry isn't needed there.

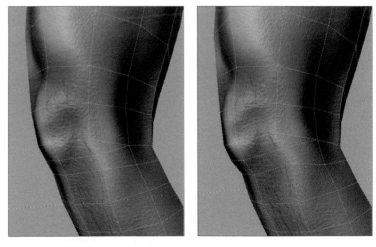

**Figure 10.53** To finish, refine the shape of the knee cap.

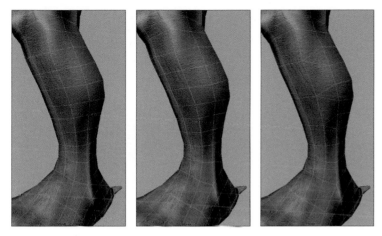

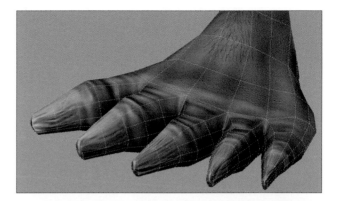

**Figure 10.54** Collapse the edges at the shin to optimize the lower leg.

We can do this quickly by selecting three separate rows of edges (see Figure 10.54), making sure not to select all the way around the leg before collapsing them.

Finally, we will look at the foot. In general, the foot seems OK, so we won't dwell on it too much. We can, however, remove a few polygons from the claws.

As demonstrated in Figure 10.55, selecting and deleting the middle edge loop from the claws leaves them almost the same.

That's the Ogre refined and optimized. The work we have done isn't immediately obvious, but that's the point. Optimization should be something that is invisible, noticeable only in the amount of processing power the model takes.

The refinement we have done is also subtle, but you should be able to look at the comparison in Figure 10.56 and see the differences. The newer model is smoother and will deform in a much more natural way, and it is more efficient with its topology.

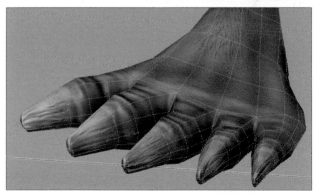

**Figure 10.55** For the feet, optimizing the toes should be sufficient.

**Figure 10.56** The Ogre before and after refining and optimizing the model.

Although this is a much better model, it has come at a cost. Before we began, the polygon count was just over 6,260 polygons, whereas now it has gone up to 7,470. We have added well over 1,000 polygons, and we aren't finished yet. If you refer back to Chapter 4, you will see that the overall budget for this guy is 15,000 polygons, so, looking at it that way, we are still way under budget, which is great!

Before we move on, there is one more thing to discuss. This may not completely apply to this model because of its clothing and so on, but the majority of game models need to be seamless. By this I mean that the characters you will work on in the future will have to be one continuous mesh, so the geometry for the arms

must be adjusted and connected to the torso, for example, the legs connected to the lower shirt…and so on. This is important mainly for animation because having open elements can cause major problems. As a rule, I would make all your models this way, unless specifically asked not to, or unless elements need to remain open.

We have one more chapter to go before the Ogre is complete. Next we will finally give him some eyes and hair and add the missing accessories.

# 11

# Modeling the Extras

With the Ogre's base model complete, refined, and optimized, we can now focus on the details and create the missing pieces for this model. In this chapter we will generate the belt, eyes, and shirt details while exploring alternative ways to generate normal maps.

## Eyes

The focus of any model or living creature is its eyes. When we interact with people we are drawn to their eyes, and the same is true when watching them on screen, so they are important to get right.

Early game characters didn't have the luxury of separate eyes, so they were simply painted into the face texture. As time moved on, and more detail was needed in facial animation, the eyes became simple spheres with the ability to rotate as the character surveyed its surroundings. Now the gaming public demands more. With machines becoming ever more powerful, we are relying more on the systems' real-time engines to help us tell our stories, so in-game facial animation is paramount. To this end, we need realistic-looking eyes, not just in how the texture looks but also in how lighting reacts with them (see Figure 11.1).

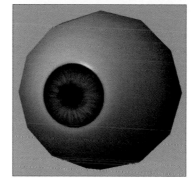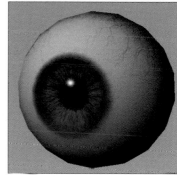

**Figure 11.1** In this example of an early and a current eye model, you can see the differences in detail and lighting.

In this section we will generate a realistic eye, like the one in Figure 11.1, which we will use on the Ogre, and which you can also put aside to use on future models.

### Eye Anatomy

Before we begin building, its, important to look at how a real eye is constructed. We will then break it down into basic parts before building our own real-time eyeball.

Look at the diagram in Figure 11.2, which shows the basic anatomy of an eyeball. For the purposes of this exercise, I have left out the areas with which we are not concerned.

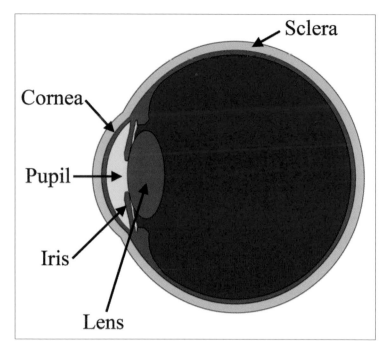

**Figure 11.2** The basic eye anatomy.

Light travels through the cornea at the front of the eye. It then passes through the pupil, whose size is controlled by the iris, and into the lens. The lens then adjusts the image and focuses it onto the retina, which passes it to the brain along the optic nerve.

Although this information is useful, all we are concerned with is how the eye looks, and what we can see when we look at one. From the outside we see the sclera and cornea, which make up the main bulk of the eye. The cornea needs to be transparent so

that we can see the iris and pupil through it. So essentially we can create two pieces of geometry—one for the outer eye and another for the areas seen through the cornea.

We also need to consider how light reacts with each surface. We need the outer eye to be as smooth as possible, while also making sure the curvature of the cornea is evident. And we need to replicate the concavity of the iris so it catches the light across its base. To help in both these areas, we will use normal maps, not only to create the smooth surfaces but also to add subtle details like veins and grain to the iris.

## Outer Eye Modeling

Now that we have a basic understanding of the eye, we can start building. To begin with, let's look at the outer eye.

Your eyeball is essentially a sphere, but we only ever see the front (that is, unless your character's eye needs to come out of its socket). Because of this, and our need to keep the polygon count down, our final eye will be only half an eye, but initially it helps to create it as a whole.

1. Start by creating a basic sphere like the one in Figure 11.3, which has 20 subdivisions both along and around its axis.

2. Switch to the side view and, following Figure 11.4, move the vertices out to the front to form the cornea.

Now we can use this basic mesh as our in-game eye model. Next we'll create a normal map to make it appear smoother while also enhancing the cornea.

1. Rename this model "Low" and duplicate it, calling the new model "High."

2. Hide the "Low" model for now and apply a smooth to the "High" model (see Figure 11.5).

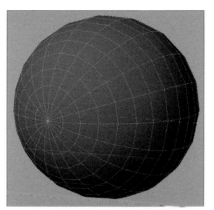

**Figure 11.3**

Start with a basic sphere.

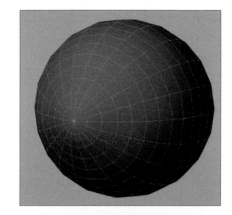

**Figure 11.5**

Duplicate and smooth the eye model to generate the source mesh for our normal map.

**Figure 11.4**

In the side view, manipulate the front to create the cornea.

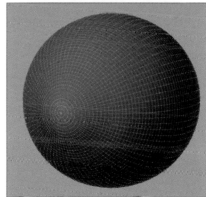

3. Now we have a lower target mesh and a higher source mesh from which we can extract a normal map. Before we do that, we need to fix the UV data on the lower model, so apply a planar projection to it from the front. Your UVs should look like those in Figure 11.6.

4. So that the normal map doesn't get confused by the front and rear UVs, overlaping, we can delete the back of the eye. This is shown in Figure 11.7.

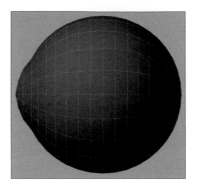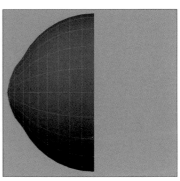

**Figure 11.7** Remove the back half of your low-resolution eye so the normal map doesn't get confused.

5. Now it's safe to extract your normal map. Figure 11.8 shows the geometry without and with the extracted map applied. As you can see, the cornea is much more evident in the second figure. But we also have a problem. When the mesh was smoothed, it created a pinch at the front—a nipple of sorts—that will ruin the eye.

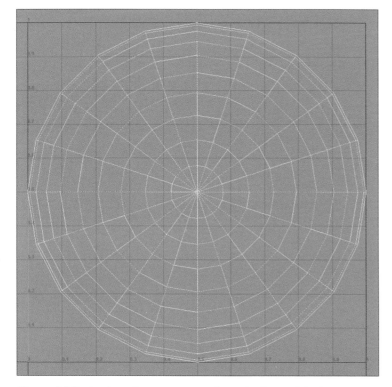

**Figure 11.6** Apply a planar projection from the front of the low-resolution eyeball.

**Figure 11.8** The low-resolution eye with the normal map applied helps to enhance the cornea, but we have also developed an unwanted nipple.

6. As illustrated in Figure 11.9, if you look at your extracted normal map, the problem area is noticeable, although it is very subtle. This is both a good and bad thing with normal maps, as the slightest color variation can have big results.

7. Fortunately this is easy to fix. Simply blur or smooth the area in your favorite 2D application. As you can see from Figure 11.9, this initially looks incorrect, but remember this is your higher-contrast version. Removing the contrast gives much better results on our normal map.

> ### Tip
>
> If you find you are having trouble seeing the pinch, temporarily adjust the contrast on your image, as per the second pane of Figure 11.9.
>
> If you are using Adobe Photoshop, you can easily adjust the contrast by using an adjustment layer. This allows you to see the problem area and fix it. All you need do is delete the adjustment layer when finished to get back your normal map.

8. Reapply the normal map to your model, and you will see, as shown in Figure 11.10, that the pinch has gone. Figure 11.11 shows the same eye but on a shiny surface, similar to a real eye.

That's the outer eye complete, apart from texturing, which we will look into later in the chapter.

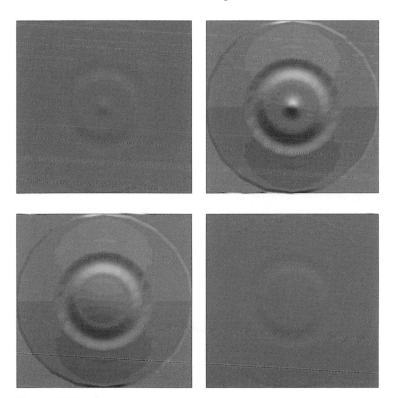

**Figure 11.9** Temporarily alter the contrast on your image to better see the problem area before you smooth it.

**Figure 11.10** With the new normal map applied, we have successfully removed the pinch.

**Figure 11.11** The eyeball with a shiny surface applied.

# Iris Modeling

Time to look at the second part of the eye we will need to create: the iris. This object will live inside the outer eye model and will be fully visible, so it has to look right. To help us, we will use another normal map.

1. Following Figure 11.12, start by creating a standard cylinder but make sure it has the same divisions as the outer eye. This way the vertices will match when we position it inside the eye.

2. Divide the cap twice before deleting the back of the cylinder. We need only the flat front for our iris.

3. The central area will act as your pupil, so adjust its size appropriately.

4. Finally, take the middle polygons and extrude inward to create the pupil.

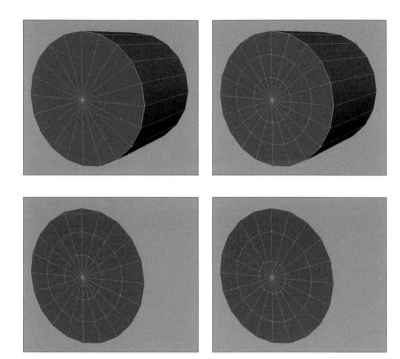

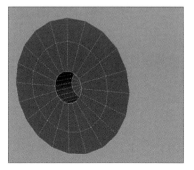

**Figure 11.12** Create the basic iris shape.

Now we have a basic iris shape. From this we will generate high- and low-resolution versions that we can use to extract a normal map.

1. If we applied a smooth procedure to the current model, the pupil would disappear. Because of the topology, the smoothing algorithm would average the pupil's entrance, blending it into the iris. To help retain the shape, we will bevel the edge around the pupil (see Figure 11.13). By adding these polygons, we will keep the overall shape.

2. Next we need to add some shape to the flat iris, so pull the pupil back slightly, making sure you also tweak the surrounding edge loop.

**Note**

The iris comes in many shapes and sizes depending on who, or what, you are making it for. Some may be convex, so adjust it accordingly at this stage to fit the destination character.

3. It's time to apply a smooth, but, before you do, create a copy of the basic model and put it to one side.

4. Hide the smooth version of the model and bring back the basic iris.

5. Now we will optimize the lower model, since we really don't need all this detail. As demonstrated in Figure 11.14, begin by removing the pupil.

6. Now remove one of the edge loops so you are left with only one to help give the iris a little shape.

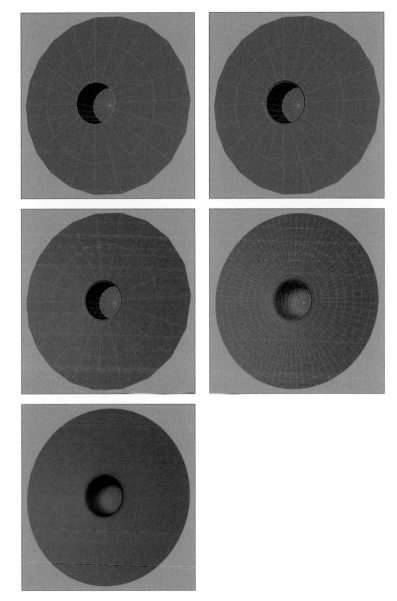

**Figure 11.13** Bevel the entrance to the pupil before you smooth the mesh.

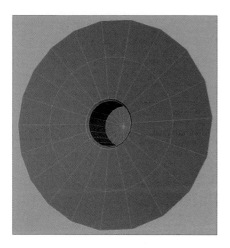 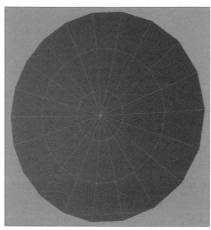 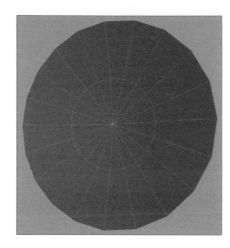

**Figure 11.14**

Optimize the low-resolution iris to create the target mesh for your normal map.

7. Next, as we did with the outer eye, apply a planar projection to the low-resolution iris.

8. However you prefer, use these models to extract a normal map. When you reapply the map, you should end up with something that resembles Figure 11.15.

It looks good, but we are faced with a similar problem to the outer eye. The pupil normal map has jagged, polygon edges baked into it. We will adjust the texture to smooth out the pupil.

Take the normal map you baked out for the iris (Figure 11.16) and smooth the pupil. You shouldn't need to adjust the contrast; the rough area is obvious.

  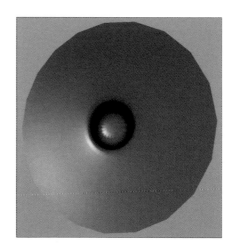

**Figure 11.15**

The normal map applied to the low-resolution iris model.

**Figure 11.16**

Smooth the pupil area on the normal map.

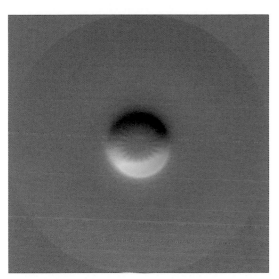

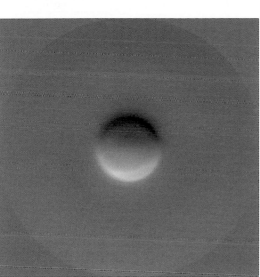

After reapplying the normal map to our model, you can see from Figure 11.17 how smooth it is looking, with no hideous, obvious polygons. The eye still doesn't look correct because your pupil is really a hole and shouldn`t catch the light, but we can reduce this later in the chapter with the use of a specular map.

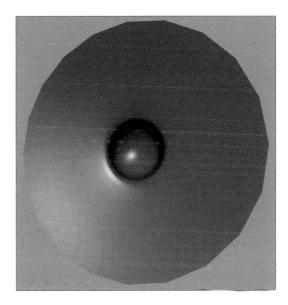

**Figure 11.17**

The edited normal map reapplied to our iris.

## Base Materials

Before we continue to the next section and add detail to the eye in the form of textures, we will apply some basic materials that will guide us and help complete this section.

The first thing we need to fix is the iris visibility. At the moment it is hidden behind the cornea, but a simple alpha map will help reveal it.

1. Start with the outer eye normal map. We will use this to help guide where we place the transparent part of the alpha map.

 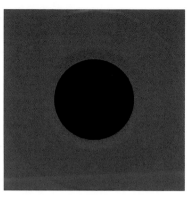 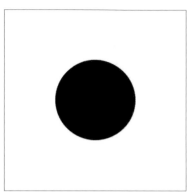 

**Figure 11.18** Use the normal map to guide the placement of the cornea alpha map.

2. Following Figure 11.18, create a large, black circle that covers the area of the cornea.

3. Fill the remaining, outer area of the texture white.

4. The circumference of the cornea isn't harsh and solid, so blur the texture slightly to soften the edges.

Applying the alpha map will now allow you to see the iris, and judging by Figure 11.19, it needs some minor adjustments to look correct.

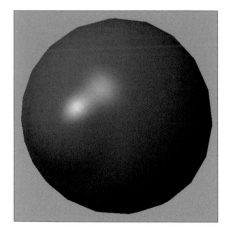  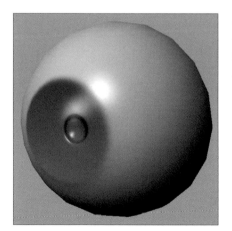

**Figure 11.19**

Once the alpha is applied, adjust the position of the iris.

Now let's look at the iris texture.

1. Load the iris normal map into your application of choice.

2. Using the normal map as a guide, create a black circle that covers the pupil area (see Figure 11.20).

3. Finally, fill the background in a different color—brown or green will do for now; we can tweak it in the next section. Adding this to our iris gives it some much-needed color.

That's the basic textures applied (see how they look in Figure 11.21), so let's move on and add some detail.

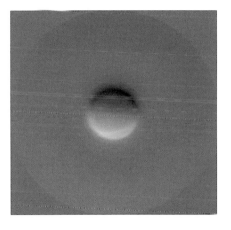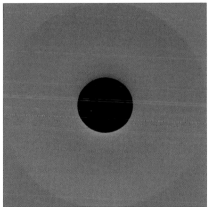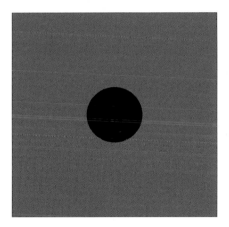

**Figure 11.20**

Create the basic iris shape.

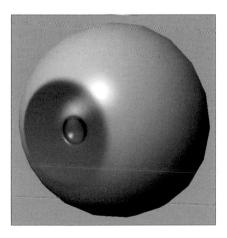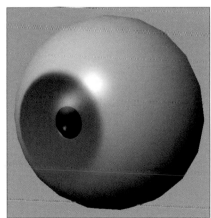

**Figure 11.21**

The real-time eyeball, modeled with basic textures applied.

# Detail Texturing

Eyes are complicated things, so trying to recreate them can be tricky, particularly the texture. Let's concentrate on the outer eye before we paint the iris detail.

## Outer Eye Texture

The white of the eye isn't simply white. Look closely and you will see many veins and subtle details across its surface. Recreating these is quite easy.

1. Load the current outer eye material into the painting application.

2. This image should still have the black circle we created earlier in its alpha channel. We need to duplicate this and bring it into our main RGB channels as a layer. Having the alpha visible will help to tell you which areas of the texture will be visible so you don't accidentally paint on the cornea, which is transparent.

3. Start by painting broad strokes, each moving in toward the center. If possible, use a brush that will automatically fade as you paint to taper the line nicely.

4. Next, with a finer brush, start to add more veins. You may also want to adjust the transparency slightly (see Figure 11.22).

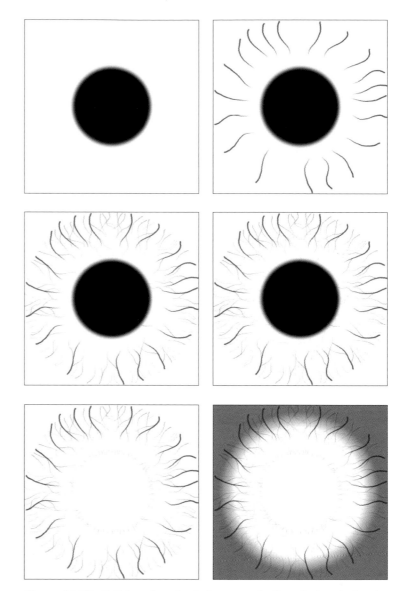

**Figure 11.22** Build up the veins in layers, gradually reducing the brush size and transparency.

5. Finally, go even finer and paint the final, outer vein pass. Again, vary the transparency because these veins exist deeper inside the eyeball.

6. The last step in adding the veins is to paint some coming out from the cornea. When you are happy with the veins, hide/delete the alpha layer.

7. The veins are looking good. You can continue to add more detail if you wish. One final thing to add is a slight gradient, moving out from the center of the eye to make the back pink. It's important that this goes onto a different layer because we will need the main veins for our normal map.

So how does the eye look so far? Figure 11.23 shows us the texture applied to the eye model. It's looking quite convincing, but we can use a normal map to help bring out some of the veins.

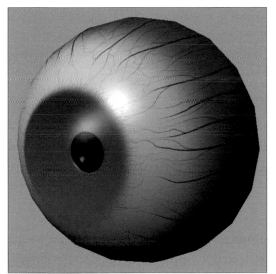

**Figure 11.23**

The eye model with the veins applied.

So how do you generate a normal map from a texture? Surely we have high- and low-resolution models? Ideally we do since that produces far superior results, but for something like this we can use one of many applications that convert a simple texture into a normal map.

The application I will use is NVIDIA's Adobe Photoshop plug-in, which you can download from http://developer.nvidia.com/object/photoshop_dds_plugins.html.

This plug-in takes your texture and treats it like a height map (white is higher), and from this it can generate a basic normal map. It has lots of options to let you tweak the outcome depending on the source texture, so it can handle pretty much anything.

Figure 11.24 shows the results of the NVIDIA plug-in applied to the veins of the Ogre's eye.

The plug-in gives a quick, cheap normal map that is ideal for this area. All we need to do now is combine it with the original normal map for the outer eye (using the Overlay layer in Photoshop works well), and we are done. As you can see from Figure 11.25, this has given the eyeball some subtle surface detail.

That's the outer eye complete, so let's look at texturing the iris.

> **Note**
>
> As mentioned in Chapter 8, Crazy Bump gives far superior results to the NVIDA plug-in; you can find a version of Crazy Bump on the companion CD.

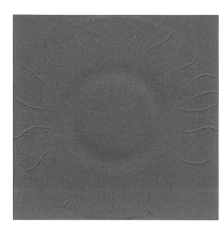

**Figure 11.24**

The real-time eyeball, modeled with basic textures applied.

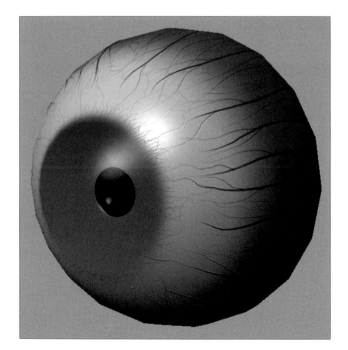

**Figure 11.25** With the normal map applied, the veins have gained some subtle lighting detail.

## Iris Texture

If you Google "iris," you will find plenty of images—some useful, others not—of eyes close up. If you examine the actual iris, you will see that it is built up of what look like hundreds of tiny veinlike strands called stroma. These move out from the pupil to the outer iris (or root), with their color being dictated by minute pigment cells called melanin.

We can use this information to help compile our texture. Since the stroma appears to be built up, layer upon layer, of the tiny strands, we can replicate them by also using layers.

1. What we need is some basic detail to start us off, so first load the iris texture you created earlier.

2. Following Figure 11.26, create a layer behind the pupil and fill it with noise, but make sure it is black-and-white noise.

3. We don't need the whole texture filled with the noise, so make a circular selection out from the pupil and discard everything outside it.

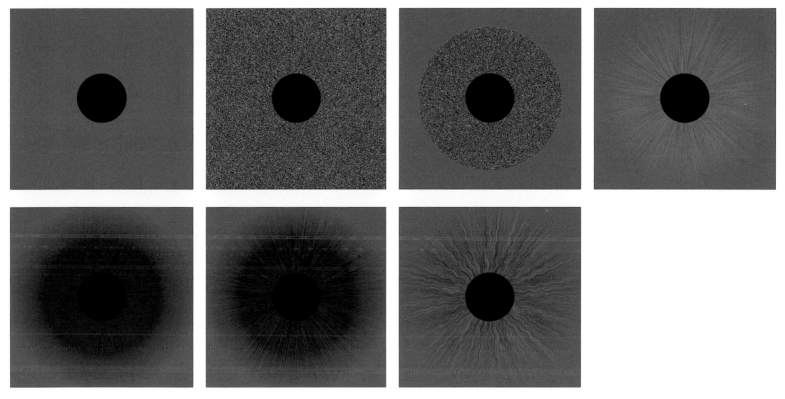

**Figure 11.26** Use the built-in Photoshop filters to create the base detail for the iris.

4. Now apply a Radial Blur filter to the layer, and use the Zoom option to spread the noise out from the center. (If you are not using Photoshop, play around with the blur options available to you.)

5. Change the layer filter to Multiply and tweak the contrast to bring out some of the detail.

6. Finally, apply a Zig Zag filter to add a wave to the layer. (If this option isn't available, experiment with other filters to try and achieve a similar result.)

With the base layer in place, we can now work on some further details that will add the layer effect we need. You can see the following steps in Figure 11.27.

1. Initially hide the base layer so you can see as you work.

2. Using a yellow color, start to create wave strokes coming out from behind the pupil.

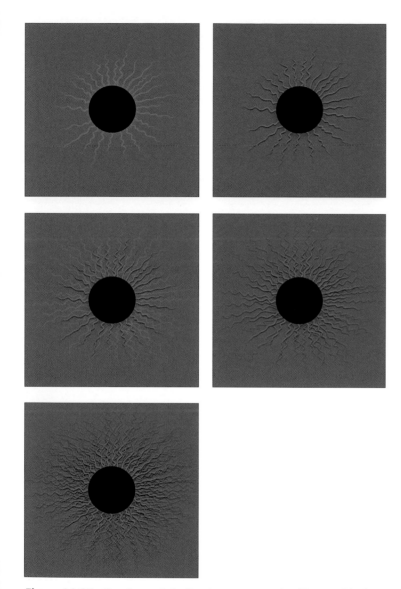

**Figure 11.27** Creating and duplicating just a couple of layers adds the built-up, layered effect of the stroma.

3. When done, apply a drop shadow effect to the layer.

4. On a separate layer, now add more strands, this time slightly thinner and longer.

5. Again, apply a drop shadow effect to this layer too, to add depth.

6. If you duplicate and rotate these layers, you will start to see the detail build up, which is exactly what we need.

Now that you have the main details in place, you can play around with the colors. As shown in Figure 11.28, adjust the background and foreground colors to suit the color of the eye you wish to make. To add further depth and detail, duplicate a few more layers, putting them behind the rest while also making them darker.

We aren't finished yet; we still have a few more steps to go.

1. The pupil is a little harsh, so first blur it slightly to soften its appearance.

2. Bring back the base layer you created initially (with the Radial Blur effect). Move this so it lies above the other layers and set the layer filter to Multiply. Doing this adds more detail to the iris, particularly around the pupil.

3. We want to break up the overall appearance now. If you are using Adobe Photoshop, create a clouds layer (Filters > Render > Clouds). If not, you simply need a layer that has a soft cloudlike look to it with varying light and dark patches. See Figure 11.29.

4. Again, change this layer type to Multiply to vary the iris color further.

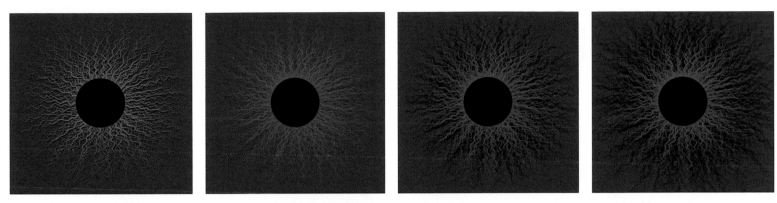

**Figure 11.28** Adjust the colors to suit your needs and add more, darker layers to the background.

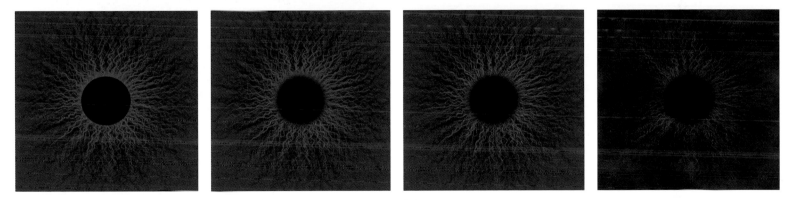

**Figure 11.29** Using the base layer and a cloud layer, you can vary the colors of the iris.

We are on to the final steps now, as we only need a few tweaks to complete this texture. First we need to add a shadow to the outside of the iris (see Figure 11.30). A simple circle cut from a black layer will do, blurred to soften the edges.

Finally, to add a subtle splash of color, we will create a soft band around the pupil.

1. First create two soft circles around the pupil, like those in Figure 11.31. Make them yellow for now.

2. Use a wave filter, or something similar, to vary the shape.

3. Finally, alter the layer filter, changing it to Multiply or Overlay so the yellow bands add a subtle color change to the iris.

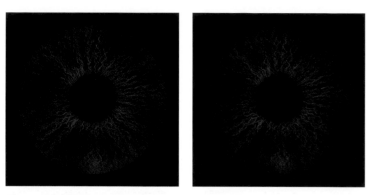

**Figure 11.30** Add a shadow to the outer iris.

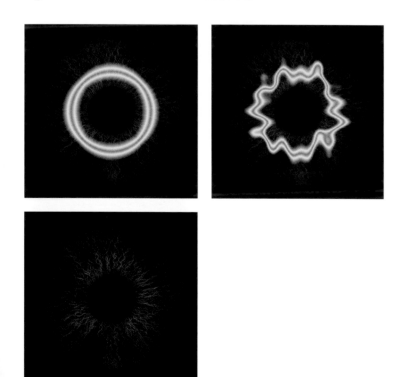

**Figure 11.31** Create a band of yellow to vary the iris color.

That's the main iris texture complete. Figure 11.32 shows it applied to the model.

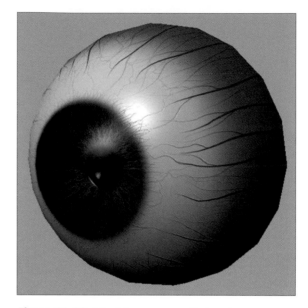

**Figure 11.32** The iris texture applied to the eye.

What else can we do to the eye? Well, for starters we can use a normal map to add detail to the iris, and we also need to sort out the specular problem on the pupil.

Let's create the normal map first.

1. Remove all of the main variation layers you created so you are left with a plain iris texture (see Figure 11.33).

2. We'll use the NVIDIA normal map plug-in again (or Crazy Bump), so to help achieve better results, desaturate your texture.

3. Once the plug-in has been applied, overlay the new texture on the existing iris normal map.

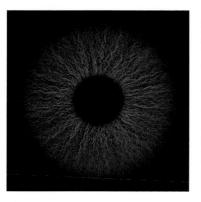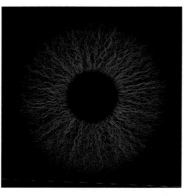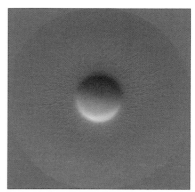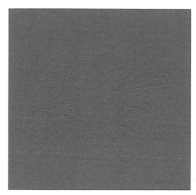

**Figure 11.33** Use a desaturated version of the iris to generate a normal map.

Figure 11.34 shows the iris with the normal map applied. As you can see, it enhances what was originally quite a flat surface.

The final stage is to apply a specular map so the pupil is no longer shiny. This will also tone down the overall iris, helping to soften its appearance. In the previous step, we created a desaturated version of our iris, which you can see again in Figure 11.35.

In Figure 11.36 you can see how applying this to the specular channel of the iris material has removed the unnaturally shiny pupil and also softened the lighting on the iris itself.

**Figure 11.35**

We can use the grayscale version of our iris as the specular map.

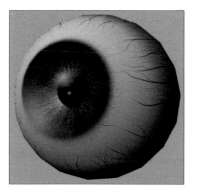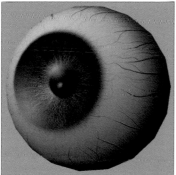

**Figure 11.34** The iris normal map comparison.

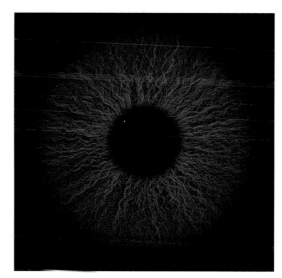

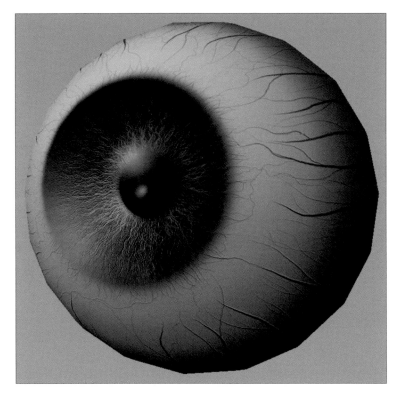
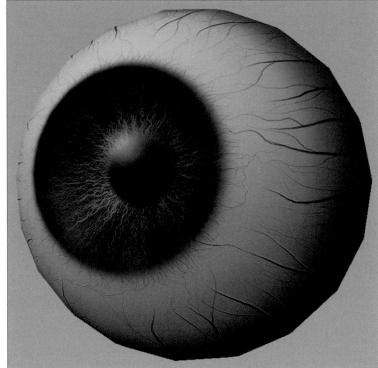

**Figure 11.36** The iris with the specular map applied.

## Eye Tweaking and Fitting

Now let's revisit the eye topology and shape. With the tweaks completed, we can finally add these to the Ogre and see how they look.

First we can optimize the eye a little. Much of the back of the eye will be hidden most of the time, so we can safely remove a couple of the edge rings. You can see this illustrated in Figure 11.37.

Next we need to look at the overall shape. At present the pupil looks too large, so rework the shape of the back of the eye, scaling up the vertices to make it larger (see Figure 11.38).

All that is left to do now is put the eyes into our Ogre model (see Figure 11.39).

Spending the time to create good, believable eyes is a must, and the bonus is that these eyes can then be used again on another model.

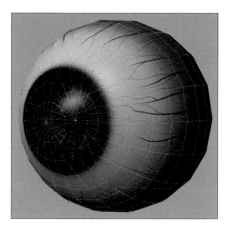 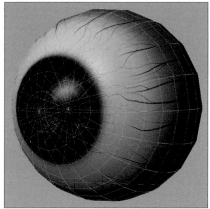 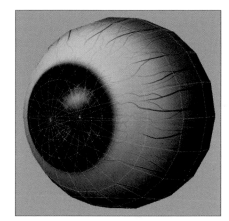

**Figure 11.37**
Optimize the eye model by removing three of the rear edge rings.

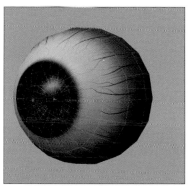

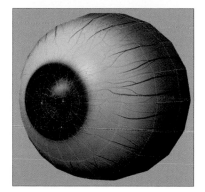

**Figure 11.38**
Correct the proportions of the eye.

**Figure 11.39** With the eyes in place, the Ogre is starting to look complete.

# Belt, Buckle, and Straps

The next elements we need to create are the belt and buckle, and the straps around each arm. And while we are at it, we might as well create the beads in his beard and his earrings. But first we need to move the eye textures we created before onto the main shirt page. This way we will know how much space we have to play with.

1. Begin by loading the Ogre's shirt texture page.

2. Delete the lower half of the loin cloth. This isn't actually used on this model, because the cloth is mirrored, and removing this half is good because it will free up some space for the accessories. You may also find that the area above the loin cloth can be cut too.

3. Your texture page should look like that in Figure 11.40, nice and clean. Bring in the eye textures next, positioning them in the lower left corner.

4. The area inside the neck of the shirt would be perfect for the belt buckle, so create a temporary circle here to earmark the spot.

**Note**

Remember to also add the relevant eye textures to the normal map and specular map, ensuring they are in exactly the same position.

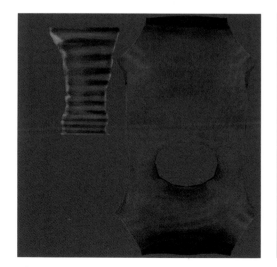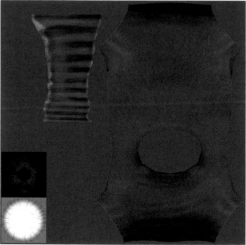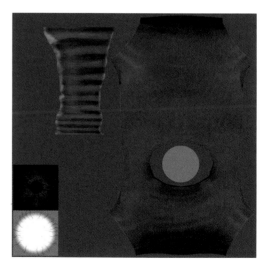

**Figure 11.40** Start by cleaning up the texture page and bringing in the eyes to claim their spot.

With the eyes in, you can now see how much space you have to play with. Apply the new texture to both the Ogre and his eyes, adjusting the eye UVs accordingly.

Moving into 3D now, we will create the belt straps and the buckle, which are quite basic shapes.

1. Following Figure 11.41, create a basic torus primitive.

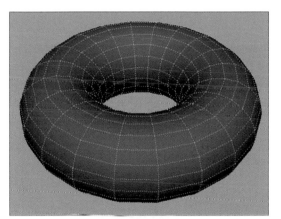

**Figure 11.41**

Use a basic torus as the base for the belt.

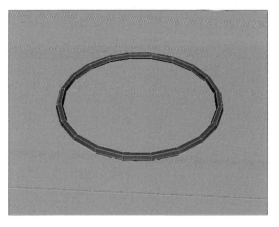

2. The default torus may not be what we need, so adjust the settings so it has 20 divisions around its axis and 6 around its height.

3. We will never see the inside of the belt, so delete the inner polygons (see Figure 11.42).

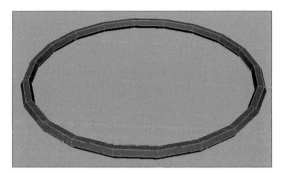

**Figure 11.42**

Remove the inner polygons as they will not be seen.

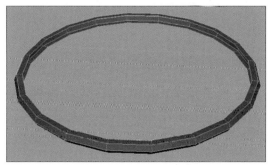

4. Hopefully, when you created the torus, a nice set of UVs would have been applied by default, similar to those in Figure 11.43. If not, apply the UVs now using any method you prefer.

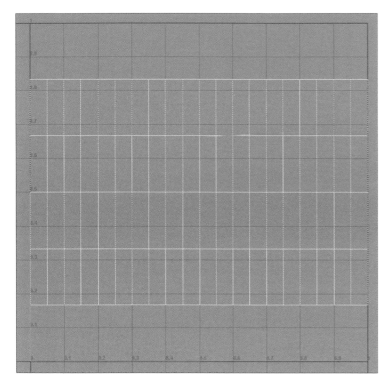

**Figure 11.43** By default your torus should have a good set of UVs.

5. Finally, for the belt we just need to position the torus, making sure it fits comfortably around the ogre's waist. As demonstrated in Figure 11.44, duplicate the torus to make extra loops of rope.

**Figure 11.44**

Position the torus around the Ogre's waist.

As you come to work on the sleeve straps, you can see that we missed an area when we refined the model. The sleeves are angular, a problem that will be exacerbated by the rope. Following Figure 11.45, divide the polygons around the sleeve and smooth out the shape.

Duplicate the belt straps and create two for each sleeve. Your Ogre should be looking like the one in Figure 11.46.

As you can see from Figure 11.47, the buckle can be constructed from a simple cylinder, scaled and moved into place, with its back removed.

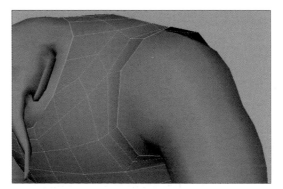

**Figure 11.45**

Smooth out the jagged-looking sleeves.

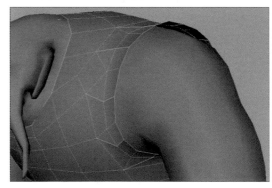

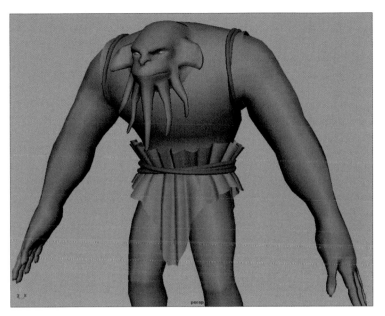

**Figure 11.46** The Ogre now has the rope belt and straps in place.

Before you texture the belt and buckle, you need to position the UVs. For the rope, you can cheat a little and use the same space for each strap. You can do this because the rope will be quite dark and therefore won't suffer from not having lighting detail applied individually.

1. First scale the UVs so they are more in proportion with the actual straps, remembering that you are doing this for all of them at the same time, so be sure you select all the UVs.

2. We will leave the space on the left for the hair, etc., so move the UVs across to the right side of the shirt (see Figure 11.48).

3. Next apply a planar projection to the buckle before tweaking the UVs and positioning them over the circle you created earlier (see Figure 11.49).

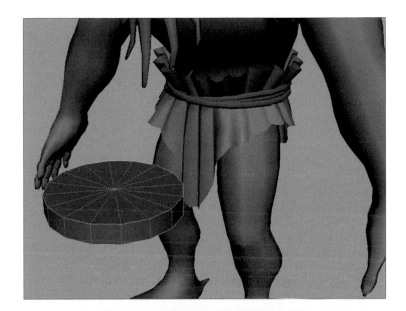

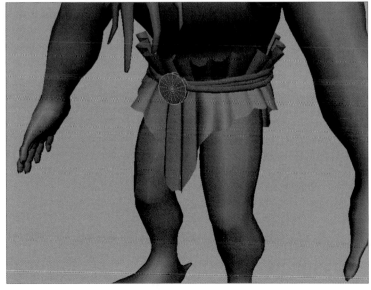

**Figure 11.47** A simple cylinder can be used for the buckle.

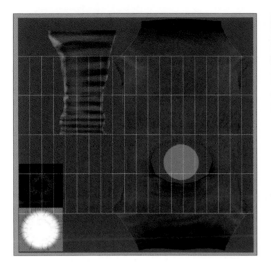 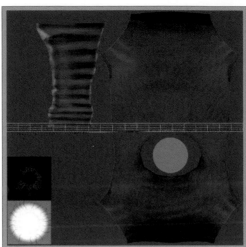 

**Figure 11.48** Scale and position the strap UVs on the texture page.

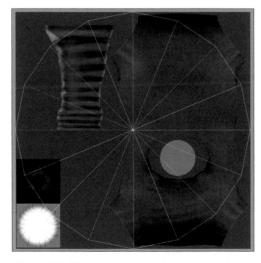 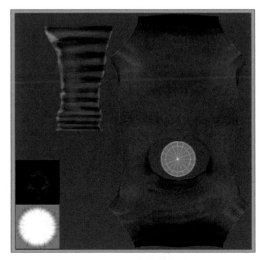

**Figure 11.49** Apply UVs to the buckle and position them.

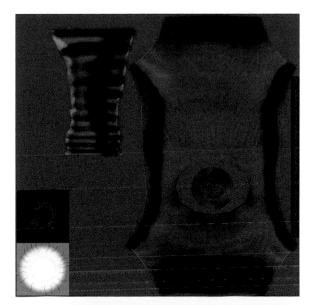

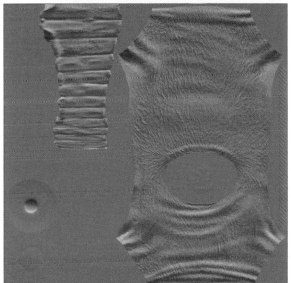

**Figure 11.50** Update the texture page and normal map.

With the UVs in place, you can now work on the textures. Figure 11.50 shows the updated texture page and normal map. You will also notice that, with the help of an occlusion map, we have added shadows where the ropes lay, adding further depth to the texture.

Figure 11.51 shows the Ogre with the new elements added, and textured. Don't worry if you aren't completely happy with the textures; you can spend time later tweaking them until they look as you wish.

**Figure 11.51** The Ogre with the belt and straps added.

# Hair, Fur, and Cloth Detail

At present the Ogre's hair is a little flat and unrealistic. We also have a problem with the current sleeves, because they need to look frayed. With the use of alpha maps and polygon strips, we will build up the hair and shirt detail to give it volume and make it look much better than it does currently.

We will create the textures first before we turn to the model.

1. We should have plenty of space on the shirt texture page for the hair, etc., so start by loading in the texture file.

2. On a separate layer, start to work on different hair configurations. As illustrated in Figure 11.52, start with a base color before working in darker, then lighter, strokes. Try to create varying patches to cope with the different areas of the Ogre: the hair on his head and on his arms, his eyelashes, and the frayed edges to his shirt.

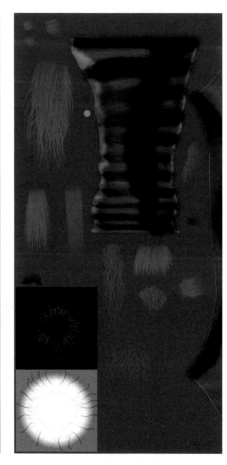

**Figure 11.52**

Build up different hair configurations.

3. We now need to update the alpha map, so duplicate the hair layer.

4. Desaturate it before adjusting the brightness and contrast (see Figure 11.53).

5. Finally, add this to the existing alpha map, placing it in the alpha channel of the texture.

Now that you have the texture, you can move back into the 3D package and start working in the hair. As shown in Figure 11.54, you first need to create separate strips for each piece of hair, making sure to divide some of the larger pieces so they can be shaped.

 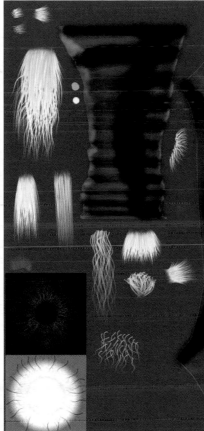 

**Figure 11.53**

Generate an alpha map from the hair layer.

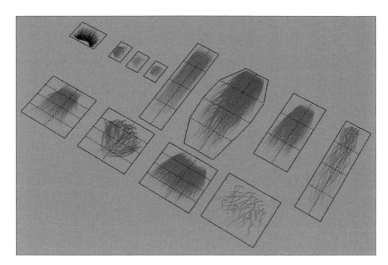

**Figure 11.54** Create a polygon strip for each piece of hair on your texture.

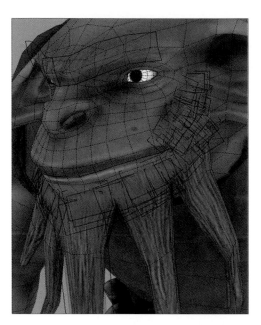

**Figure 11.55**

Start by
building up
the hair for
the beard.

As you can see from Figures 11.55 through 11.58, it's now just a case of duplicating the appropriate polygons and building up the hair. This can be a time-consuming process, but the effect is worth it.

In addition to these areas, feel free to add eyelashes and add hair anywhere else that needs it.

You may find that the hair on the head doesn't blend smoothly with the hair in the strips. To fix this, simply open up your texture and apply one of the larger hair strips to the hair, blending it in slightly (see Figure 11.59). Now the hair will look more natural as it blends from the hair strips to the head.

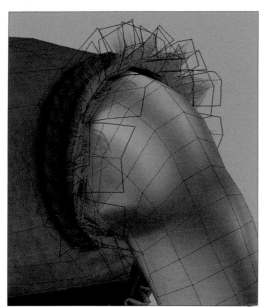

**Figure 11.56**

Next, use different hair strips to add the frayed edges to the sleeves.

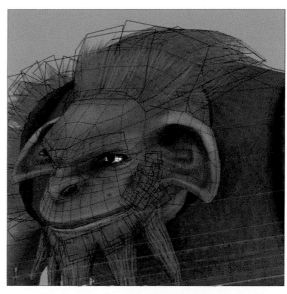

**Figure 11.57**

Using larger strips, build up the hair on his head.

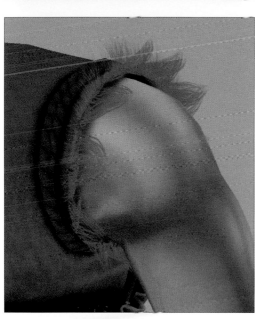

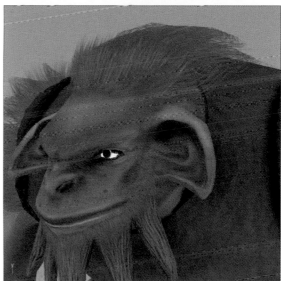

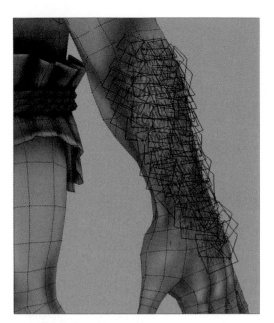

**Figure 11.58**

Continue adding hair to the arms and legs.

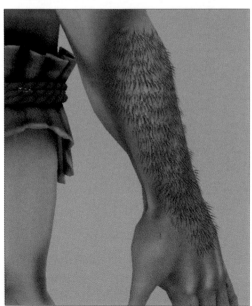

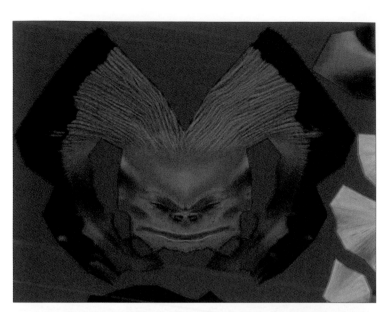

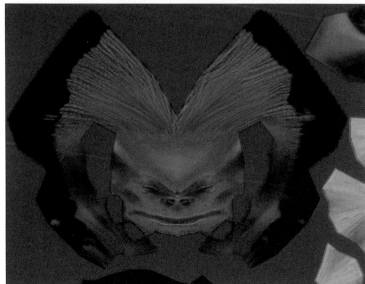

**Figure 11.59** Use the new hair texture to blend in the hair on the model.

The hair is now more or less complete; you can see the current model in Figure 11.60. Adding the hair has increased the polygon count, so we are now looking at around 11,110, but we are still under budget.

Figure 11.60 shows the unlit version and the fully mapped version. Figure 11.61 shows a render. The hardware render of the hair has some problems, but this is just an issue with my graphics card, Maya's renderer, or something else; the model will look fine in a game engine.

**Tip**

To help add depth and detail to the hair, consider generating a normal map for them.

**Figure 11.60** The Ogre with hair applied.

## Finishing Touches

Before we can sign off this character as complete, we still need to add the final accessories. As the beads and such are simple objects, I will step back and let you work these in on your own.

Additionally, it's worth revisiting both the texture pages and the model. Check for other areas to work on, smooth, or optimize, and if you like, work more details into the texture pages.

If you have time, it's always worth giving your work a polish.

Now that our work is complete, what's next? In the next and final chapter, we will take a look at the possible future of our model.

**Figure 11.61**

The Ogre final render.

# 12

# What's Next?

Your model is complete, but where does it go from here? In this, the final chapter, we will take a brief look at what happens next to the Ogre.

## The Pipeline

You have spent what could be three weeks working on this character. You have sculpted him, tweaked him, and polished him. But you can't sit back just yet; there is still work to do.

Of course, you have probably created a nice render for your portfolio, like the one in Figure 12.1, but before he goes anywhere near a game engine, there are more steps to complete.

1. First you would be required to generate levels of detail (LOD) models from this one. These are lower-resolution versions that will be displayed when the character is in the distance.

2. Once that is complete, it would be time to create a basic skeleton. Initially this is good for testing how the character deforms, but ultimately this will be his main skeleton that will be used to animate him in game.

3. Trying to animate this skeleton can be difficult, so a full character rig is needed next. Adding controllers and IK

(inverse kinematics) to the base skeleton makes it much easier to animate, much like a puppet on strings. You are simply adding the strings.

4. We will need the Ogre to emote, so facial expressions are important. First he would need an inner mouth created before a full set of blend shapes. Blend shapes are copies of the head that are posed in various positions, whether expressions or simple phonemes. These are then linked back to the main head, which can then morph between them to give the illusion of animation.

5. The last stage, usually when the game comes to crunch time, is further optimization. When the game isn't running at top speed, it's usually time to reassess the in-game assets and reduce the polygon count and/or the texture pages.

These areas are all covered in depth in my first book, *Game Character Development with Maya,* and all of the methods are still current and used today.

So I guess it's time to say thanks for joining me on this journey. I hope you have learned something from this book. Happy modeling!

**Figure 12.1** A portfolio render.

# Appendix

## Resources

This appendix contains a list of essential resources for any game artist.

## Websites

The four Websites listed below are part of the same company, and each offers excellent reference photos, textures, and even game models. There are subscription fees that range from about $24 per month to $150 for a year, but in my opinion they are worth every penny.

www.3d.sk/

www.human-anatomy-for-artist.com/

www.female-anatomy-for-artist.com/

www.environment-textures.com/

Another great resource for those with funds available is the growing library of DVDs from Ballistic Publishing. These hold around 300 high-resolution images of human references in various states of dress and a wide variety of poses.

www.ballisticpublishing.com/dvds/

The next link is the gallery of Marcus Ranum. This is a female-focused site that has some great clothed and nude reference photos, and they're free.

www.ranum.com/gallery/index.php

CGTalk is an online forum I use regularly, and the following thread was set up to help point people toward references found on the web.

http://forums.cgsociety.org/forumdisplay.php?f=202

Not necessarily an anatomy site, The Blueprints has a wide range of reference images ranging from characters to vehicles.

www.the-blueprints.com/

## Books

The Internet is an amazing resource, but there is something to be said for having something real that you can refer to. The great thing about books is that you most often get high-quality images, many of which cannot be found on the Internet and usually come with helpful tips and tutorials.

I couldn't move on in this section without mentioning my first book, *Game Character Development with Maya*. If you're looking for what to do next with your Ogre, this book will help you create levels of detail models, and rig and animate him. Although it is dedicated to the Maya user, many of the techniques can be translated to other applications.

www.ant-online.co.uk/GameCharDev/index.htm

In addition to their great DVDs, Ballistic Publishing also has an ever-expanding library of digital artwork books. Not only are these great for reference and inspiration but they also showcase some of today's top CG talent.

www.ballisticpublishing.com/

They have also produced a series of tutorial books centered on various aspects of digital, and traditional, artwork. All of which are essential additions to any game artist's library.

www.ballisticpublishing.com/books/dartiste/

As you can imagine, the world is full of reference books covering all aspects of anatomy. I cannot list them all here, so I will let Amazon do the work for me with its great review system.

# Forums

Here are some popular places to showcase your work, view other people's work, and ask for help if needed.

http://forums.cgsociety.org/

www.gameartisans.org/

www.subdivisionmodeling.com/forums/

www.tweakcg.com/

# Tools and Applications

Finally, following is a quick list of links to many popular tools and applications that many artists use on a daily basis.

Silo
www.nevercenter.com

Autodesk – 3D Studio Max, Maya and Mudbox
www.autodesk.com

Adobe – Photoshop 7, Illustrator
www.adobe.com

Crazy Bump – Image-based normal and ambient occlusion map generation
www.crazybump.com

X Normal – Normal, ambient occlusion, and parallax map-extraction tool
www.xnormal.net/

# Index

# License Agreement/Notice of Limited Warranty

**By opening the sealed disc container in this book, you agree to the following terms and conditions. If, upon reading the following license agreement and notice of limited warranty, you cannot agree to the terms and conditions set forth, return the unused book with unopened disc to the place where you purchased it for a refund.**